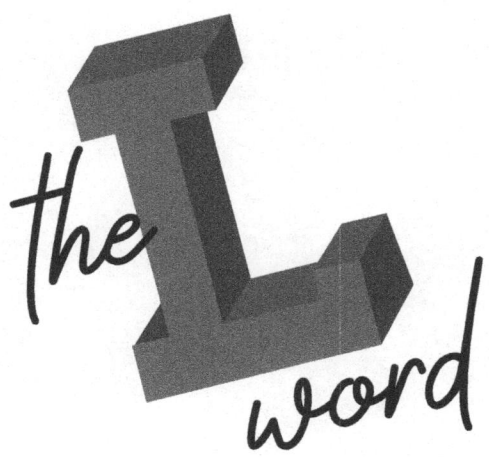

the L word

LOVE, LUST AND EVERYTHING IN-BETWEEN

AASTHA ATRAY BANAN

HarperCollins *Publishers* India

First published in India by
HarperCollins *Publishers* in 2021
HarperCollins *Publishers* India, Cyber City, Building 10-A, Gurugram,
Haryana – 122002, India
www.harpercollins.co.in

2 4 6 8 10 9 7 5 3 1

First published in Ebury Press by Penguin Random House India 2017
Copyright © Aastha Atray Banan 2021

P-ISBN: 978-93-5422-476-8
E-ISBN: 978-93-5422-477-5

Typeset in 11/15 Palatino at
Manipal Technologies Limited, Manipal

Printed and bound at
Repro India Ltd.

HarperCollins *Publishers*, Macken House, 39/40 Mayor Street Upper,
Dublin 1, D01 C9W8, Ireland

For all the listeners of Love Aaj Kal,
*and Ankit, without whom these conversations would have
never happened.*

Contents

SECTION 3: RELATIONSHIP SAGAS

SECTION 4: LOVE AIN'T ALWAYS EASY

Introduction

Ever since I started my podcast on love, 'Love Aaj Kal', I have realized two things: Love is a universal emotion; and two, also a universal problem. Young people, and older, are all wondering about how we find love, how we hang on to it, and how do we get by without it. And somehow, even when we truly know the dos and don'ts (as I truly believe we are born with innate good sense and judgement), it's always good when someone spells it out for us. For example, I have learned a lot from the bestselling book, *The Secret*, and I often remind myself of the teachings in the book: 'believe and you shall receive'. The same way, I feel that when a relative stranger (aka me, in this case) tells you some hard truths about love, you nod your head and say, 'Yes, this makes sense'. Maybe you won't follow the advice entirely, but just maybe, you will remember it here and there, and maybe make wiser choices. Or at least choices that hurt you less.

Love is to be enjoyed, and love is meant to be healthy, and love is meant to make you more YOU. Especially in 2021, we have realized that when life is so transient, do we have time to waste on bad love? No; a firm NO!!!

So, read on, and as I talk about all the common questions and dilemmas about it, maybe you will relate to it, and maybe you will find some solace, and some direction. Maybe, you will just store away the information for later use.

Whatever it may be, what I do hope you take away from it is that love is meant for all of us – all we have to do is keep our hearts, minds and souls open to it. And of course, make an effort.

Best of luck and may the 'love' be with you

Lots of love,

Aastha

SECTION 1
Virtually Yours

Dating has become a sport and not about finding the person you love.

— RASHIDA JONES

1

Take a swipe on me

(As Harshad Mehta said in Scam 1992,
risk main hi ishq hai)

When I was twenty-one, the dating pool consisted of school friends, later college friends, then brothers of friends, friends of friends, and finally, when you finally started working, other interns who were slogging it out just like you. If you were 'fast' – or promiscuous as it was called in those days – you had a fling or two with your thirty+ boss. Don't roll your eyes. It was 2002 and at that age even the obviously unhappy, dysfunctional, dealing-with-his-own-demons older man looked exciting and sexy.

But I am digressing. The year 2021 is a very different place to be if you are dating, trying to fall in love, or find someone who will be with you for the rest of your life; even till the end of the year might work. In the last few years, the game of love has changed ever since dating apps came trotting into town. It's now all at your fingertips, and let's face it, it is all about that hot picture, convenience of location, or the witty answer to some inane question like, 'dating me is like ...' or 'I am weirdly attracted to ...'

It's only much later in life do you understand that compatibility is never about easy questions like this. But before we get that far, let's talk about the mad, toxic, exciting, sexy, insecure world of dating apps.

Let me give you an example. I am sitting with my two best friends from work and we are talking about their experiences on Tinder. These are an accumulation of the many, many experiences I have heard in the past few years.

Take this: Girl swipes on boy. They indulge in some instant banter. Move to WhatsApp. Decide to meet. Great date. Sleep together on the first date. He even cuddles! (Oh, how perfect of him). He spills his guts and tells girl about the fact that he is in therapy. Girl is overwhelmed with emotion – he must like me, she thinks. Boy texts two days later – his therapist has asked him not to sleep with the girl anymore and to end it, as he may like her too much! He is not ready for this mentally. Girl is angry. Boy feels bad, and visits her, and then sleeps with her again. But sorry, therapist's orders. And so, he is gone. This time, forever.

When my friends and I sat down to talk about this guy, my first question was why he slept with her in the first place, since his therapist wanted him to focus on his life. Moreover, why was he even on a dating apps?

Good sense and experience made me believe he was lying to get out of subsequent dates. But maybe, he also wanted to not look like a bad guy. He couldn't break up thinking my friend would believe he was a fuck boy. Instead, he wanted to vanish. What he did offer as an explanation was this: He couldn't keep away from my friend even though he was in therapy, and after he realised she was getting serious, and conveyed that to his therapist – she told him to cool off before the girl got even more involved. That comes across as brutal, but maybe it's good it ended earlier than later.

Let's take another example:

Boy meets girl. Girl is hot. Girl and boy hook up. Best sex ever. But chemistry fizzles out. Girl and boy break up. Girl says she is totally fine with it. But girl now starts talking to boy's exes. And friends. And family. She is now best friends with everyone he knows. Boy doesn't know. One day, boy comes home, and finds the girl at the reception – she just came by to say 'Hi!'

Yes, sounds like your classic Hollywood stalker movie, but this is real life.

Here's another example, and this is one of many DMs I received on Instagram. An eighteen-year-old met a guy on a dating app. They talk morning, night, and all the hours in between. He sends her a good morning text, and a good night text. As the lockdown lifts, they make plans to meet on Friday amidst much excitement. On Thursday, she texts him to figure where they should have dinner. There is no answer. There is no answer on Friday. There is no answer on Saturday. There is no answer ever.

Every experience is more bizarre than the next. But then, what does one do? Dating apps are the only legitimate place to meet anyone anymore!

I think it's clear that even though we don't know why people behave the way they do online; heartbreaks happen all the time. Failed relationships or failed online meet-cutes hurt everyone and perhaps it makes it even more important that we be more responsible. Yes, the anonymity helps, but can we leave people better than we found them? Especially in a world where we anyhow are slammed with everything that promises to break us.

A lot has changed in the dating scene. It's not like in 2003, when I was sitting in Hawaiian Shack, a retro bar in Bombay's coolest suburb, Bandra; a time when people sent over drinks. Despite being an obvious overture of desire, it was alright if one didn't kiss them or sleep with them. But yes, you could have a lovely conversation with them. Of course, if you didn't like them, you could always gulp your drink down and tell them you had a curfew time. But then you may get caught at the next bar which was open till 5 a.m. and bump into everybody from the previous bar over there. Ah, the good old days!

But these days, why would anyone risk hurting their ego by asking someone out with a drink at a bar? Isn't it always better being rejected on a platform where no one else can see you wincing and crying?

And so, everyone and their ex is on the apps.

Dating apps seem like a parallel world where singles, and wannabe singles, live in a continuous loop. People meet, insanely optimistic about where this could go, start getting panic attacks at even the first thing that goes wrong, and soon one ghosts the other, and we are back to the drawing board.

'What's baffling is, why instead of ghosting, they can't just tell you they are just not into you. Why lead you on? Why say I love you to get sex? Why not be honest,' says a sweet friend of mine, who just wants it straight. More on this very-millennial concept of ghosting later.

But then, as I think about it, most humans have never been good at being straight. It would take the drama out of life, and what's life without some drama? Sigh.

But as an astute piece, 'The Five Years That Changed Dating' by Ashley Fetters, in The *Atlantic* from 2018 said, many people getting married or engaged in these times met on a dating app. A Manhattan therapist to young couples actually commented that if he asked couples how they met, most of them looked at him like a fuddy-duddy. Their answer was always: 'on a dating app. How else does one meet?' As of this year, according to a study by businessofapps.com, Tinder has 57 million users around the world. Bumble has 12.3 million users per month, and Badoo (not in India yet) is the largest in the dating app world with almost 500 million users.

Sean Rad and Justin Mateen, two of Tinder's founders, have said in interviews that the inspiration for Tinder came from their own general dissatisfaction with the lack of dating opportunities in real life – or, as Rad once said, 'Justin needed help meeting people because he had, what's that disorder you have where you don't leave the house?' As Mateen said in the same *Time* magazine interview in 2014, 'Nobody joins Tinder because they're looking for something.' Rad went on to say, 'They join because they want to have fun. It doesn't even matter if you match because swiping is so fun.'

Or as one smart twenty-five-year-old single man told me, 'Dating apps haven't change the game. They have just brought it closer home.'

Well, in the world we are now living, where a pandemic could strike us anytime, cloistering us in our homes, it would seem to say Justin's words were prophetic.

What it goes to show could be that even though the way we look for a partner has changed, the need to find a sexual or emotional partner is the same. The challenges may be greater though as now along with the general menu of pros and cons a relationship has to go through, singles these days – as my co-podcaster on 'Love Aaj Kal', Ankit Vengurlekar, puts so succinctly – also have to deal with the 'illusion of choice'. The fact that there is someone maybe more attractive, better-suited to you emotionally, better in bed … all at the swipe of your finger.

As 30-year-old journalist Prutha Bhosle, who has been on dating apps for five years now, says, 'But it makes sure we don't lose hope. If one thing doesn't work out, we can say, "There are more fish in the sea". It keeps me hopeful. I can't meet people organically – my job gives me no time, and I am very comfortable in my circle of friends … so how will it happen. On the apps of course!' Then she muses, 'But Ankit is right. Even if you meet someone you like, he may be ready to ghost you, as he is done, and has more choices.'

Jyotsna Mohan Bhargava has observed young people very closely, especially for her book, *Stoned, Shamed, Depressed: The Secret Lives of India's Teens*. 'I think it's very casual. But then again, when very young people are dating, casual is the key word. The problem is it's all very transient, and millennials have lots of choices. They don't even have friends that last for years, how can they have relationships. They don't believe in working on things – it's all about moving on. Sometimes that's very good, sometimes bad.'

And this choice of plenty begets bad behaviour. For Bhosle, the worst part about the apps is that since they know they can 'maybe' find someone better, people don't put effort into their relationships. 'So, you have to keep starting over. Every time, answer questions – where did you go to school, what do you like eating … blah blah. It's like an interview. It gets superbly monotonous.' But, as Harry Reis, PhD, Professor of Psychology and Dean's Professor in Arts, Sciences, and Engineering at the University of Rochester, said in a paper he wrote on online dating: 'There's the old saying that you have to kiss a lot of frogs to find a prince – and I think that really applies to online dating.'

And so, there goes the one big advantage: the dating pool is almost as large as the sea itself that you look for 'plenty of fish' in.

So, since we are living life on the apps, why not make sense of it. And why not take inspiration from people who have met on the apps, and landed up married, or even better, in a fulfilling relationship that requires no labels. Yes, it's a utopian world, but if we don't imagine it, who will?

First things first: be clear about why you logged on.

The two thirty-year-olds I spoke to, a man and a woman, both said that the best thing about the dating apps is that it saves time.

'Be it sex or relationship or marriage ... know your purpose', said the girl.

'It really saves time. So be as clear as you can be about what you want!', said the boy.

World masters have talked about the art of manifestation. If you know what you want, and can see it clearly, and believe it, you are bound to get it. And that could work on apps as well, right?

So then, it best that you know why you are there in the first place.

If you want a one-night stand, or sex without strings, just say so – and believe so – then maybe you will only attract that tribe.

And if you want a relationship, then only think of that while talking to someone. Be very, very clear.

In fact, this clarity could help you choose the right app as well. Maybe an app that stresses on conversations and relationships, instead of one that talks of dating more causally. Bumble is good for women who want to make the first move and are confident enough to do so, OkCupid has the most detailed questionnaire so you know more about the person you swipe on, MeetMe is for people above 40, Happn is for women looking for men, Her is for women looking for women, Coffee Meets Bagels offers icebreaker questions and gentle nudges to respond to those messages waiting in your inbox – perfect if you're a bit shy, Ship lets your friends weigh in and decide a match for you as well, Hinge is for people who want to move one step above Tinder, and Feeld is for people who want to have polyamorous relationships. Phew, and that's not even the half of it – choice of plenty!

Most people on the apps, who write in, lament how they can't understand why they are not able to find the person they want, or the ones that they did ghosted them after two dates. My suggestion to them is always: get your own heads on straight first, know exactly why you are on the app, make it clear, be honest, and then move ahead. That will give you much higher chances of finding someone.

'The best thing is it saves everyone's time. And heartbreak. And drama,' says Bhosle and we agree.

2

How to swipe away

(Don't worry if it doesn't happen the first time – there is always more fish in the sea)

'You can't get clingy on an app, or spend too much time on one person when it's not turning out the way you wanted. Let go!' a thirty-one-year-old, rather self-aware, good looking male writer tells me.

His suggestions are brutal but effective, and quite clear: 'Take two steps back, one step forward. Don't be too quick to express what you are feeling, and be coy. Be distant till you feel a comfort level, but don't wait too long. Don't be pushy and move on soon.'

But moving on, in these times, usually involves 'ghosting' – a term every millennial is scared of. It means just vanishing into thin air, but only for the person who you were once talking to/sleeping with/dating. On one hand, you could be posting pictures on Instagram as you actively block someone on WhatsApp on the other. A twenty-eight-year-old wrote to me about finding out that her lover, who had told her was thinking about getting serious with her, blocked her one day and put up a post about dating someone else instead.

But most of us hate conflict or the reality of actually explaining to someone why you don't think you two fit. But trust me, not ghosting someone could clear the path for you and for the other person involved, and in the process lighten everyone's load.

You may think ghosting isn't a big deal, but as I have heard singletons spill their guts to me, ghosting is a big problem for everyone. It leaves us alone, abandoned and without an answer to our questions. As therapist Shefali Batra told me on the podcast, 'Speaking about it always dilutes the trauma.'

So, if you tell someone exactly why you feel the way you do, or why you did what you did, they understand you better and empathize. Otherwise, you have just left them with a hundred questions and most of them will turn into doubts that will feed their insecurities.

To make sure people don't ghost, we need to bring some accountability to dating apps, and that can only come from you, the user.

As psychologist Jennice Vilhauer said in an article on ghosting in the *New York Times*, 'It's really important to remember if someone ghosts you, that behavior says more about them than you. It's about *their* discomfort. You have to keep trying.'

I agree.

3

When you call and call and call ...

(and nobody picks up)

Q. What is ghosting?

Answer 1: That guy or girl doesn't find you attractive anymore and decided to look elsewhere.

Answer 2: Now that you both have already slept together, he doesn't see any use in calling anymore.

Answer 3: Maybe she found you boring, and that's why she has stopped responding to your messages.

Answer 4: She found someone better-looking than you and maybe she isn't interested in meeting you anymore.

Answer 5: They got scared because you showed your feelings too much, too soon?
    etc, etc, etc ...

According to Urban Dictionary, ghosting is 'when a person cuts off all communication with their friends or the person they're dating, with zero warning or notice before hand. You'll mostly see them avoiding the friend's phone calls, social media, and avoiding them in public.'

But according to my personal dictionary, ghosting means you were once with a person who doesn't have a backbone.

Like my mentor, and *Sunday Midday* editor, always says, 'I need a man with a spine.' I think we can just replace man there with 'person'.

A person with a spine doesn't ghost.

So, let's go back to what a lot of you might consider the Stone Age – maybe 1999–2003?

I was young and dating, and broke up many times with many different men. Did any of them ghost me? Or did I ghost either one of them? No, didn't need to. We just never saw each other again, thanks to the fact that there was no Instagram or Facebook then.

But breaking up was a ritual. You had to have 'the chat'. You had to give back the stuff they bought you, and they had to return the stuff you left at their home, car, office. You would cry a bit, and ask through the tears, 'Whyyyy?' A break up didn't feel complete without the drama.

But these days, all everyone wants is no drama. They want to vanish in a world where it's so hard to vanish (thanks to social media), and pretend they were never with you. Pretend you don't exist, so that they don't have to even acknowledge the pain they may have caused you. If you don't exist, like a ghost doesn't (usually), then there is no responsibility that exists.

What's worse is that the party that is 'ghosted' feels like they did something wrong. And they don't get closure.

But let me tell you one thing. Closure is often overrated and nobody can give it you, other than you to yourself.

It is something I have also learned the hard way. I once had a book deal, where I was going to write a book about a famous person. I was ecstatic – this was my big break. Two years after working on the book, the publisher called me one day and said, my writing wasn't working for them, and I wasn't getting what the 'famous person' was all about.

Now, this wasn't good enough. I wanted them to explain to me why I wasn't good enough. I wanted closure. But I didn't get any. Not a message, not an email. And so, I cried for one day, had one drink too many, and then the next day, I forgot I ever had a book deal. I ghosted my pain.

So here, I would say one thing, and it's true: It's not about you, it's about them.

In a *New York Times* article, which quotes Gili Freedman, who studies the language of rejections at St. Mary's College of Maryland, says that Dr Freedman discovered ghosting has a lot to do with how we feel about our future – or whether we think our mate is the 'one', which is a question of belief versus destiny. 'Individuals who have stronger destiny beliefs are more likely to ghost,' she said. 'If you're with someone and you realize they're not the one for you, you're going to think it's not much of a point to put in the effort, so you ghost. These people believe relationships are either going to work out or not.'

I don't know exactly when ghosting started. The internet says somewhere around 2006, but we know now that it's common. People even ghost friends, sometimes even work!

But since we are living in a world where ghosting is a done thing, then why not be prepared for it, and figure the signs soon enough.

Let me give you an example.

A girl I knew was in love. She flitted around at work, left early for long dates, and was finally putting happy selfies on Instagram.

A boy was taking her out, drinking wine with her, having long conversations with her, sleeping at her home, in her bed, with her, and was not leaving once he was done. This had to be it.

Then one day, he started delaying plans:

Let's meet tomorrow.

Maybe day after?

Let's meet next week?

Then, he started avoiding her calls and messages.

She started going crazy.

People at office noticed the difference. Gone were the smiles, instead the smoke breaks increased.

Then one day, she asked a colleague, who had a friend who was friends with the 'guy', to check if he was still alive! After all, how could he vanish like this.

He was alive. He just didn't want to explain to 'girl' that he didn't just feel it anymore.

Phew, so long drawn out!

He was just not that into her, though you could have been fooled to believe he was!

This isn't just one of the horror stories.

Let me tell you another one.

Girl dates guy.

They date date date, and then go out for New Year's to her friend's home.

Her friends love her. He feels appreciated and wanted.

This is it, right?

She stops calling. She messages once a day, that too when he messages her. She posts stories on Instagram, even as she ignores him.

It's over, right?

So, here it is.

A man or a woman (who you are dating or romantically interested in) is more likely to ghost you, if:

- **They avoid having an argument or fighting.** This inability to have a confrontation – healthy disagreements are essential to a good relationship – means they would go to all lengths to avoid anything that might be unpleasant to them.

- **There are no detailed conversations about the future**: even if they tell you, they love you.

- **They don't tell you about their past**, for this may reveal something about them that they might not be comfortable with.

- **They often miss your calls and cancel plans**, with excuses such as they slept off, or they have family commitments. The excuses get hazier with time.

These four statements or warnings should be enough.

But since people without spines are usually not open to taking advice, here's what you can do if you do get ghosted.

- **Unfollow them** everywhere possible. So that when they are done ghosting you, well, they can't find you!

- **Channel your frustration** by creating some kind of art – bad as it may be.

- **Focus on not ghosting yourself**. Be kind to yourself. Love yourself. Get a haircut. Buy a new wardrobe. Go for a run. Eat good food. Drink good wine. And then instead of thinking about them when you are drunk, sing along to Beyonce's *Sorry*: 'Middle fingers up, put them hands high, wave it in his/her face, tell him, boy, bye (girl)'.

- **Forget, but don't forgive**. That way, you won't again. Forgive yourself though, so you can move on.

- **Don't ever let it make you feel** like you didn't deserve a proper good bye.

It's not you, it's them.

4

Did it even happen if it's not on the 'Gram?

(Insta-official and all)

I am often left wondering how couples on Instagram take the selfies where they are in bed sleeping, and both their eyes are shut. Who took the selfie? Are they paying a photographer to take a picture as they sleep and make it look like it's a selfie? Or are they taking it themselves? How do they know what button to push on the phone or camera? Questions, questions, questions.

It's the age of social media, and as my podcast co-host, Ankit always tells me, 'If it's not on Instagram, did it even happen?' Of course, it did.

Remember the 90s? When there was only one wedding album and lots of envelopes full of photos developed from camera rolls. Those weren't uploaded anywhere, and those events still happened. So why do we need to show off on Instagram now?

Well, I think the only reason something like this may mean something is if you want to be very sure that you are not in a relationship your SO is hiding or isn't that sure about yet!

A secret relationship is when either one of you is not comfortable going public yet. It could be if you are having an affair, or if you don't want your work colleagues to know (if office dating is frowned upon), or if you don't want your parents to find out. But if it's any other reason – because of how a person looks, talks, walks, or just because you want to weigh your options, or because you want to play the field a bit more, and may have other lovers on the side – well, then it's a big no-no.

In all of these scenarios, your lover will never go Insta-official with you.

Signs to watch out for if you think you may be someone that your lover is hiding …

- **They never post about you**, neither in their stories or posts.

- **They never like** any of your pictures, or leave comments.

- **They bristle every time you post** about them, and get into a fight, and say things like, 'Why can't we keep this private?'

- **They post about everything else** in their life – from what they ate to their dog to their best friends – freely and in abundance.

If these points are true, you are truly in a secret relationship. And the best way to deal with a secret relationship (if you are the one who doesn't want it to be a secret) is to end it.

An article in *Psychology Today* said that '… higher relational secrecy was associated with reduced self-esteem and negative personal health. He notes that other research corroborates the fact that secret-keeping, in general, has a deleterious effect on wellbeing, and that romantic secrecy, in particular, may pose a personal health threat, because it causes partners to feel bad about their relationship.'

Of course, it will lead to anxiety, fear about the relationship ending abruptly, and constant stress that tomorrow you may wake up and find yourself alone. And then people might say, 'What did you expect? He didn't even put up a picture with you. Couldn't you read the signs then?'

Well, even if you couldn't then, now you can. Five steps to end a secret relationship:

- Start your day with self-love affirmations. Remind yourself of your worth. You are an amazing person – and why should anyone hide you? If you don't believe you are amazing, how will anyone else?

- Ask yourself, do you need the anxiety? Wouldn't you rather use all that energy to do something productive in your life?

- Make a clean break. Block. Disconnect.

- Date other people. Be open to it. See what a difference that makes.

- Know that if it was a secret, it probably didn't mean much. Don't take that as a personal offence but think of it as another reason to move on without too many tears wasted.

But here I also want to say something more.

Being Instagram-official is not the be-all and end-all of a relationship. You don't need to be in every picture, and every post, for the relationship to matter. There are many relationships that are thriving even when they are not on social media. My own husband, who is a private person, will never be found on my Instagram unless it's his yearly birthday post. 'I am not comfortable with my life being on a public platform. We have a life that we live together. I think that's more important than showing love on social media. We share love every day, at home.' That's what he had to say when I asked him if he felt odd about his absence on my social media.

We will be married fifteen years this year.

Social media validation as a couple isn't everything. Just notice the signs that form a fine line between someone being a private person and someone who is hiding you. Be aware.

5

It does work out

(Love might just be hiding behind that click – there is proof!)

Devika and Neil Patel met on Hinge right after major breakups. They had both been in long-term relationships and were in no mood to be in another. They were bored, for the lack of a better word. And so, there they were on dating apps. 'We both made it clear from the beginning that we weren't looking for anything serious,' Devika tells me, and laughs, 'And look where that got us!'

What strikes me is that at least they were honest with each other, and maybe that reciprocated honesty helped them move closer. After one-and-a-half years of dating, they got married in December 2019, and it's been exactly what they wanted. 'We spoke the truth, and then, we took it as organically as we could – very slow, very steady, very cautious.'

In fact, according to 'The Knot 2019 Jewelry and Engagement' study, 22 per cent of newlyweds met online. Plus, recent insights indicate that marriages formed from dating apps may be less likely to end in divorce as members use the sites to date intentionally. Some studies also say that couples who meet on apps have the ability to communicate better, and thus, could be happier with each other. Actually, in a 2012 report on a study by the sociologists Michael Rosenfeld and Reuben J. Thomas published in the *American Sociological Review*, the researchers found that couples who meet online transition to marriage more quickly than those who meet offline. It could be, as the Tinder researchers say, because when people commit to online dating, they are actually looking for something concrete.

I also feel that if you do know why you are on an app, and are honest and don't lose hope, well, you can be sure that your time will come. Bhosle, who is still single but has seen many of her friends get married to people they met on apps, says that she has often questioned whoever she can about how they managed this feat.

'The answer is inevitably about "the time being right". I had a friend who tried dating apps for three years, but at that time she had job issues and family problems, and so she wasn't giving it her all. The day she was ready, she found someone who was as well.'

But thirty-year-old Gautam tells us he feels that usually the couples who end up getting married because of the apps, do so as they know that they have reached the end of the line. 'But they have made the best choice, and have had the best options. So, this is sort of a logical ending.'

So, it would make sense that in a world where the app playground could be the only playground one can play in, if we had to settle down, we would do it there as well. This is the real world now for many of us, especially when it comes to love and lust, and we have to live by its rules and adapt to them. Because we as humans, do it well.

To end this chapter, and give it a very Indian context, I spoke to entrepreneur Devika Patel in detail about why she thinks she found love and marriage on an app, compared to many who amble around for years. Patel told me that sometimes people don't give an app a chance and are even scared to admit they are on it. 'That works against the whole premise of the app. If you don't want to even admit you are on the app, how will it work for you? You are on it, but you are judging everyone, and everyone is judging you. I was very clear that I wanted to meet someone outside my circle – not just the same people at weddings and parties. So, I think my energy worked well, and I met some interesting people, and even my husband. It's also a little bit of luck. So, give it patience and time. Let things brew – it may surprise you – don't expect instant coffee.'

6
A valuable tip

Never be afraid to take the first step. There are many love stories which are left incomplete, or don't even start, because someone didn't want to text first. So:

- ▸ Be the first to ask someone on a date
- ▸ Text first. It doesn't matter what the outcome is
- ▸ Say sorry first
- ▸ Say I love you first

▶ Say I miss you first

▶ Say I will make this better first

▶ Say I will change first

Speak your heart, and the rest will follow.
If it doesn't, then it was never meant to be.
Trust that this is the way your life goes.

SECTION 2

That Sexual Feeling

Would you let me kiss you there,
You know, down there, where it counts?
I'll do it so good, I swear I'll drink
every ounce.

— PRINCE, AS HE SOULFULLY SANG
'IF I WAS YOUR GIRLFRIEND'

7

Sex? It's still complicated

(Jumping into bed got easy; it's the after that's hard ... and sometimes the in-between)

You would think that since we are now in 2021, sex, and all that goes with it, would be easier. No, it's still quite a mess.

Three years ago, when I first started 'Love Aaj Kal', I got a question that I haven't been able to forget. It was from a sixteen-year-old boy from Surat, who asked: 'My girlfriend and I want to do it for the very first time. Is it safe to have sex in an Oyo room?'

I was stumped. I wanted to scream out loud, 'You are sixteen, please don't have sex, and especially not in an Oyo room!' But of course, sixteen-year-olds are now having sex. So instead I told them that if they had to have sex, then they should do it somewhere they were the most comfortable and safest. And to please do use protection!'

Even forty-five-year-olds write in, confused about sex etiquette. Is it okay to have sex on the first date? Is it okay to masturbate? Is having sex without love bad? Is it okay to have sex with multiple partners? Can a woman articulate her desires? Can a man watch porn? Is it okay to be asexual?

It really hit me hard – most Indians are still confused about sex, because we talk so little about it. We may talk about our relationships with our friends, or even parents now, but how many of us are truly honest about what's happening in our sex lives? We aren't exactly like the friends from *Sex and the City*, sitting over breakfast and talking about how a guy's cum tastes funky, or how giving anal a try does not seem like a bad idea.

I don't think we even admit to ourselves what's lacking in our sex lives. Or what we want in bed. Or desire. Or lust after. Perhaps this is the reason so many of us either live sexless lives or have sex with people other than the ones we are in a relationship with. Isn't it time we started being true to ourselves?

We are stuck in unhealthy patterns when we are having sex ...

- **To feed our validation** issues
- **As toll** to keep a toxic relationship going
- **Just because saying no** is hard
- **Without thinking** about the other's pleasure
- **To get over** an ex
- **To pretend we are cool** in front of our peers

The list is long.

Much as it might seem a laughable matter, peer pressure or rather the emphasis on 'getting action' as it's called can lead to unhealthy attitudes towards sex and sexual well-being. Bhargava feels so too. 'I think they are facing immense peer pressure. They will be called prudes if they don't have sex, so they just want to get sex over with. The good thing is that sex is not on a pedestal anymore.'

Serious sex questions aside, we are not even ready to try something new with a partner if we haven't been with them long enough. And sometimes, even in long-term relationships, there isn't any communication of wants and desires. Sex is still something we rather not talk about. And if we aren't talking about it, then it's bound to create problems.

A Tinder survey from 2019 said that while a majority of young city folks are open to experimentation, a much smaller proportion is actually incorporating it into their sex lives. Only 37 per cent of single Indians feel free to experiment when having sex with someone they met on a casual date and only 24 per cent try something new in bed when in a relationship.

So yes, sex is something we can talk for hours and hours about, and yet we still spend a very little amount of time actually talking about it. So, let's change that and begin now.

Why are we scared to talk/experiment/discuss anything to do with sex?

Ask yourself the following questions to get to know yourself better:

- ▸ Do you have body confidence issues? Before we can expect others to accept us as we are, we need to accept ourselves.

- ▸ Are you afraid your partner may not take your wishes into consideration? It's time to have a conversation about boundaries and expectations.

- ▸ Do you feel you won't be able to satisfy your partner? Once again communication is key, and sharing feedback, especially the good kind is imperative.

▸ You will get pregnant. USE CONDOMS ALL THE TIME.

Sex for the first time? Or on the first date?

I really am the one who says 'wait'. Wait till you are twenty-one. Wait till you know everything about your body and know that if it doesn't work out with whoever you are, it's all good. So, wait till you know that if sex doesn't go totally the way you wanted it to, it has nothing to do with you and your 'sex skills', or the way your body looks.

That last point is very important, and I'll go out on a limb here and say, especially if you're a woman. In 2019, twenty-one-year-old plus-sized American blogger Stephanie Yeboah experienced fat-phobia, when she found out that a guy she had gone on two dates with had slept with her as a bet, for money. She received an email from his friend explaining that he had been dared to 'pull a fat chick'. That's how she ended up becoming a fat advocate. And then there is also Michelle Elman, who has had fifteen surgeries before the age of twenty. As a consequence of understanding her own perception of her body and how this was something that affected many women around her, Elman started the

'Scarred Not Scared' campaign, which champions body positivity. Later, she wrote a book, *Am I Ugly?* which is a response to the statistic that 10,000 women a month google the same phrase.

In an interview with *Dazed Digital*, Elman said, 'I think often times in the media, we are taught sex is for beautiful people and if you are outside of the beauty ideal, you will struggle to find someone who will want to have sex with you. Particularly with fat women, they are rarely portrayed as having loving relationships, or even a relationship that isn't riddled with insecurity and they are most definitely not shown having enjoyable sex. In the bedroom, I often think beauty becomes an obstacle for pleasure because a lot of people focus on maintaining their beauty. They worry about unflattering angles or sweating and it prevents them from actually enjoying the moment rather than having a conversation in their head about what they might look like.'

So ladies, listen up. No matter what, do not equate sex or the quantity or quality of sex with your body.

If it's the first date, I always tell my friends, please wait. How many men do we know who wouldn't look at a girl differently if she slept with them on the first date? How many girls wouldn't look at the boy as a player if he tried to get them into bed the first time around?

Though most of the research backed us up, HelloGiggles did a piece in 2017 that said, 'When you meet someone new, you have to make a lot of judgement calls. Are they interesting? Do they make you laugh? So why not get right to the point and see if you have sexual chemistry? Yes, sometimes the first time sleeping with someone is not *always* their best performance, but it's smart to at least get an idea of how they work in bed.'

Aaaargh. We are flawed. We judge too quickly. We lose interest too quickly. We feel that if we already slept together, why try any longer. Sometimes, we give it up all too quickly and we leave our hearts behind on the bed we may have spent only 20 minutes in.

It's just the way sex is. It can be bad. It can be good. It can be great. It can help you express yourself. It can make you question yourself. So, I would say wait till you know you can deal with s-e-x – be it for the first time, or on the first date.

If you are going to have sex – for the first time ever – either at the age of sixteen, twenty-one, or thirty, make sure you know what sex is about. Read about it, watch some aesthetic erotic film, enrich yourself, and know that it's supposed to be pleasurable and should feel good. Chances are maybe it won't feel good the first time to your body, but it should always feel good in your heart and head.

If you are having sex before twenty-one, then be careful, be comfortable, and be certain. Choose someone you really like and be certain about it. You should keep in mind that this person might not be the one you will end up with forever. Find a place you can be comfortable at and not worry about who will walk in or who may see you. And be careful: carry protection and stop at any time if it doesn't feel right. And girls, you should carry your own condoms. Always.

'Most of the questions I receive from my community on a daily basis (and I honestly receive hundreds every day) are some variant of "am I normal". The combination of societal shame and stigma along with the ensuing lack of accurate information means that most people are worried that there's something wrong with them when it comes to their sexual selves. We often pathologize our own (very normal) bodies and desires, because even thinking a sexual thought or simply seeking to access contraception can seem transgressive, let alone navigating one's relationship with porn, or seeking medical treatment for an STD.' Leeza Mangaldas, a sex-positive influencer with a wide following continues, 'At best, this results in dozens of clueless young people left to figure out for themselves everything; from how to have safe sex to how to have an orgasm. At worst, this results in things like women being killed for not bleeding on their wedding night, queer kids being sent to be "cured" by conversion therapy.'

I remember being in New York in the summer of 2018, reading *Delta of Venus* by Anais Nin on the train. Oh my god, was it a revelation. It was written in the 1940s for a private collector – because that's how erotic writers wrote back then – and it turned me on so much that I could have orgasmed on the train. The way she described it, the exotic settings, the slightly taboo tone, all made me see sex in a completely different way. I wish I had read more erotica growing up, so I understood better what pleasure was.

But it's India. We don't talk about our desires.

And that's why you use the World Wide Web in a good way. Or buy some books. And then maybe, touch yourself to figure what you like. It's just you, and you have the right to touch yourself.

When it comes to sex on a first date, well, that's a tricky one.

I always say wait. Wait till you know the person's intentions are right. Now, I don't mean that they need to marry you. They just need to be honest with you – they need to say, hey, I just want sex. Or hey, I just want you badly right now, but I don't know if I want this to go somewhere. Their intentions should be out there and at the center of the conversation.

It they are not straight with you, ask yourself what do YOU want. If you just want sex, go ahead and do it. If you want more, please wait. Only do whatever you want to do, if you are sure you will be fine the next day, no matter what happens.

The same rules will apply whenever you have sex but I have a few more pointers to really make sure you don't regret your first-time.

- **NEVER do it** to make someone like you. This applies to all of you; whether you are a 16-year-old who just wants the popular boy or girl to like them; the 21-year-old who seeks validation through sex; the 30-year-old who is being forced to settle down; or the 40-year-old who once again is seeking validation due to age-related anxiety.

- **STOP at any point** it feels off/uncomfortable/weird/forced.

- **FEEL something** for the person who you do it with – it doesn't have to be love. It could be respect, a fondness or an affection – any feeling that is positive.

- **DON'T do it** because you were drunk, and couldn't tell wrong from right.

- **DON'T expect** the other person to care about your sexual health – carry your own protection, girls and boys.

Marilyn Monroe once said, 'We are all born sexual creatures, thank god, but it's a pity so many people despise and crush this natural gift.'

But that's not what we are going to do.

Sex is a delicate enough matter, and it's best if it starts well. So why not give some thought to it before you get into it? Maybe 20 years ago, or even as recently as 10 years ago, you would have not had an avenue to do that. But it's 2021, and we can talk about it as much as you want.

In my experience of listening to love problems and figuring out where the two genders butt heads, sex is always a problem area on dating apps – and even in real life.

Most men want it quickly and easily, and most women don't want to admit they are ready to give it up quickly and easily – please note, I say 'most'.

As a 32-year-old man told me, 'Most girls think acting like prudes makes them seem like a prize. They get offended if you flirt, and, if God forbid you want to chat dirty. They are not even open to it. Isn't the point of a dating app to be more open-minded? Yes, be careful, but don't be a prude. What are you doing on a dating app if your bio says "not here for hook ups!"' He smirks wryly, 'Tables quickly turn when they want to be flirty … then they want you to respond in the same tone.'

Maybe it will do everyone good if we think just a beat before we jump into the sack. Just a beat. Hear me out?

So, if you are guy, and you think a second before you sleep with the girl you really don't have much in common with – all you like are her legs – you could think about how she would feel when you don't call the next day. Like shit, right? Then she would send you a hundred messages. Worse, she could come to office and break your coffee mug on your head. Even worse, she could call you out on social media.

Why would you want to sleep with anyone, if you wouldn't want to call them the next day. And if that's okay with you, please be upfront about your beliefs, behaviour and habits, before you sleep with anyone.

Or don't sleep with her.

Instead, you message her the truth, and move on.

If you are a girl, I suggest you think one second before you sleep with the bad boy, who you know is a bonafide f*** boy – the one who won't call back the next day – you are already doubting every word that comes out of his beautiful mouth. Think of the time you will waste later stalking him and feeling bad about yourself. Even though you know you are a queen, this encounter will eat into your self-respect.

So instead, message him, and say, it's too soon for you. And that you want to take it slow.

If he isn't good with that, you wish him well, and say goodbye.

In both scenarios, blood will not be shed.

Mangaldas sees this as an extension of educating people on love and sex. 'I genuinely believe that sex education is central to greater gender equality … and to a safer, more compassionate, more pleasure and love-filled world.'

The next chapter is when you attempt to have sex without love, which could be much more often than sex with love. Since it's such a norm, I think it's best we get right into the thick of it.

8

It's just lust, not love

(Is what you need, making you fake that loving feelin'?)

Early on, I realized that boys say 'I love you' to get what they want from girls. And that girls, who think these three words mean more than the world itself, think to themselves that if he says he loves me, then it must all be okay.

It works well; most of the time. Picture this. Girl meets boy on a dating app. Or in the building they both live in. Or in a bar. Or at office. Or through a common friend. Both are tired of all the dating stuff – pretending to get to know someone, like them, love them, have sex, and leave and start all over again. The boy just wants a girl who doesn't ask too many questions and gives him some 'action'. But he likes to pretend that he isn't like those insensitive guys; he likes to believe he is woke! So instead, he pretends to like her.

As Greg Behrendt, the author of *He's Just Not That Into You: The No-Excuses Truth to Understanding Guys*, (the movie we all watched!), said: 'We (men) would rather lose an arm out a city bus window than tell you simply, "You're not the one." We are quite sure you will kill us or yourself or both – or even worse, cry and yell at us.'

The girl, on the other hand, has had many of those men who have told her they just want to 'hook up'. So, when this nice boy, whose red flags are fading fast, keeps saying: 'I love you, and I care about you', she thinks it's okay to get into bed.

'Sex isn't good unless it means something. It doesn't necessarily need to mean "love" and it doesn't necessarily need to happen in a relationship, but it does need to mean intimacy and connection ... there exists a very fine line between being sexually liberated and being sexually used.' Author Laura Sessions Stepp very wisely explains it in *Unhooked: How Young Women Pursue Sex, Delay Love, and Lose at Both*.

That's so right.

Take this example: A twenty-three-year-old was having sex with a thirty-two-year-old man. At first, he felt like a saviour, a man who understood her mental health issues, and who wanted to make her feel good about how she looked, about how she felt. They took selfies in bed, they laughed, they smiled, and he was always around. For a bit.

Then he only came around when he needed sex, or was nice only when he was lonely. Then it went out of the window.

Another twenty-six-year-old boy wrote to me about how his sexually-active and Casanova status made sure that women just chatted him up when they needed to have sex. They actually never really thought he needed to even have a conversation.

Another twenty-nine-year-old, who slept with four men at work, and as a result felt she was taking control of her urges and agency, found herself branded the office slut. Let's keep the problematic aspect of calling someone a slut aside for an instant.

I think like anything else, when people start doing anything, including having sex, because of someone else, their status will change from being liberated to being used.

And, so, they start having sex. Till it's over. And the whole circle begins again.

Well, as much as I am an advocate for love, I think it's better to have sex for sex's sake, than for fake love.

And as I have come to know – through the podcast – and gotten shocked by, and then understood, that most millennials (or not), do have sex without love.

After all, it's just sex. It's about pleasuring yourself and someone else. It's about needs. And desires. And it's not connected to love, and neither should it be.

My problem is that even though I understand that, I still feel one person always gets hurt. Hurt when the sex stops. Hurt that the person didn't fall in love with them. Hurt when they move on to another person and get treated the same way as before. Hurt when their sexual history is held against them (never fair! But it happens to men and women both).

Okay, let me tell you a story.

Raj and Simran (no, not that couple!), madly in love, are on a vacation or staycation or just a night on the town and about. They have a drink, fool around and then sit around and play some stupid drinking games: how many people have you slept with, done anal with, talked dirty with, done positions we have never done before … oops, there it comes.

They get upset with each other because they have been with others, had experiences – all without being in love. They tell each other, it's different now because they love each other. But, one always gets upset. If you can do all the things you do with me, without love, with another, then what's special with us?

Okay, now you are reading this and calling me old-fashioned. But I am not old-fashioned, I just want less pain for everyone involved. Sex is tricky, and sex should be at least indulged in with a person who respects you

– enough to tell it as it is before it happens. So that if it's over, you still have what's most important – your self-esteem. A paper I read in *Psychology Today*, titled 'The Feeling Self: Self Esteem' had a great thing to say: it's best to indulge in physical attraction only if 'it enhances your self-esteem'.

I like to quote the famous, and some would call very scandalous, writer Hunter S Thompson, who once said, 'Sex without love is as hollow and ridiculous as love without sex.'

In all my experience of being asked the most complicated questions about sex and love on social media, one of the most common problems and heartbreaks arise when people have sex with you and then there's a disconnect. They cry, get depressed, go into an insecurity spiral, stop eating, start having sex with many more random people, hate themselves for doing it … it's a mess. Hvovi Bhagwagar, who is a practicing psychologist and psychotherapist, looks at it like this: 'Here's where age comes handy, I guess! Young ones look at sex as a checkbox, exploration, conquest, maybe even a proclamation. Dating apps and social media make hook-ups all the more easy. So yes, many millennials do try on sexual relationships like clothes, thanks to choices and accessibility.

But, the plus point for most of us humans is that as we mature, we naturally want more out of a sexual relationship-partnership, romance and fidelity. So if you don't grow out of one-night stands and hook-ups, you many need some help with your commitment levels.'

And I always say the same thing, which is what I will say now as well: It's cool to care about the ones you have sex with, and it's even cooler when they care back. It's what true 'cool' is. Like Sting and his wife Strudie, who after almost 40 years of marriage, live their life up and experiment with tantric sex together!

It doesn't get cooler than that. Really. And, if you guys don't know who Sting is, it's time to use Google the right way. If you don't know about tantric sex, then you should definitely Google it!

9

Mr and Miss Wrongs

(Also popularly known as fuckboys, and psycho chicks)

Growing up, I had no clue who a fuckboy was. Or who was a psycho chick. Now, looking back, I can see both prototypes in my own life.

Scenario 1: I met an old school friend. He was comfortable to be with, and we liked the same music. We had a few lovely months. Then, one morning, a sobbing girl called me, asking me to leave the love of her life alone. I could have anyone, so why did I choose him. Turns out, she was his ex, and she was still in his life, and he was sleeping with her when I wasn't around.

Classic Fuckboy.

Many years later, he wrote me a letter and apologized. It's the most beautiful letter ever written to me, and so I forgave him. After all, we were only twenty-one.

Scenario 2: I met the love of my life. And I also met my language of love: to be a doormat. Do everything, spend money, have no life that mattered other than the boy's. And so, he cheated on me, took my money, went off to New York to study, and cheated on me again, and then one day, stopped picking up my calls. Fuckboy.

I still haven't forgotten him. How do you forget a man you loved the most, and he loved you the least?

Scenario 3: A friend told me about a boy she was dating. He took her for granted, Cheated on her. Took her money. Lied. Hurt her every chance he got. Ignored her. Gaslighted her. (Read chapter on p. 79 for more on that). Well, you got the drift. Fuckboy.

Scenario 4: All the girls, myself included, have stalked men, stalked their girlfriends, not let them hang out with their friends, fought with them every chance they got, checked their phone, yada yada yada. You get the drift. Psycho chicks.

To be politically correct – which I really am not – I am now going to rechristian Pyscho Chicks as Miss Wrongs and Fuckboys as Mr Wrongs. *cue eye roll*

How do we spot a boy who is surely, and completely, going to be Mr Wrong? I am going to tell you how to spot them, so please remove those rose-tinted glasses and listen to me. I promise this will save you lots of heartache.

Pop culture examples of Mr Wrongs include Bunny from *Yeh Jawaani Hai Dewani*, and also Mr Big in *Sex and the City* before he turns a new leaf. But why do you need to have so many seasons of tears and therapy when you could have just been a decent guy?

For me, a fuckboy is when a man does what Bob Marley said. 'The biggest coward is a man who awakens a woman's love without the intention of loving her.'

That's it for me. But I am going to explain it.

A Mr Wrong will … (feel free to tick away below)

- **To start with, he will be handsome**, charming, and say all the right things. He will make you feel like he has been waiting for you all his life. This one is like Count Dracula – saying all the right things so that he can suck your blood.

- **Once you have been dating and sleeping together** for a while, he starts getting harder and harder to get in touch with. Phones ring again and again, and messages sit unread. When he does call, he makes it sound like it was impossible for him to get to his phone. (Even though when he is with you, the phone is his best friend).

- **Excuses are his go-to**: 'My mom was around, I was working, I got stuck in traffic, I slept off, I was tired … blah blah blah.'

- **After one point, he stops** making plans altogether.

- **Experts says a fuckboy doesn't get too personal** with you. But I have noticed they get very personal – they may even make you meet their family. But too much of a good thing, too early, is also something of concern. It doesn't mean anything. The point is they get personal with you, but they really don't care about your dreams, friends, and your everyday problems.

- **He has crazy, long, detailed explanations** of why things seem off. He over-explains everything.

- **He says 'I love you' too soon**. And has sex too soon.

- **You are nowhere on his social media**. In the world that we live in, as shallow as that sounds, it matters.

- **He ghosts you**. First, it will be a few hours, then a few nights, days, and then forever.

Now, let's move on to Miss Wrong. This one is a character too.

Pop culture examples include Blair Waldorf in *Gossip Girl* and Rebecca Bunch from *Crazy Ex-Girlfriend*. Rebecca changes cities to follow a boy, and Blair sabotages everyone she ever loves!

So, anyhow. A Miss Wrong is …

- **She calls you again and again** and again and again – lots of missed calls here – till you pick up. Important meetings or classes be damned.

- **She hates all your friends**, especially the ones from her own gender.

- **She thinks that every time you are not available** to her, you are with another girl.

- **She stalks your social media** accounts, and knows every comment, and every female follower by heart.

- **She lies** to get your attention.

- **She turns up at places** just to surprise you. 'Hi, I am your daughter-in-law.'

- **She focuses on problems**, and not on solutions.

- **She loves**, loves, loves fighting.

These kind of people are oh-so-common now a days. Poet Megha Rao told me, 'If he isn't good for my mental health, then he's Mr. Wrong. And it's the same for Miss Wrong! I think partners who are responsible, respect boundaries and support your personal growth are incredibly attractive. So anyone who isn't that, I'd avoid. Because in the end, everyone deserves a shot at being happy – and if the person you love isn't letting you do that, then you need to reconsider their place in your beautiful life.'

So, this is it, this is who they are. I am sure most of you have met them already. But sometimes, seeing it in writing, by a 39-year-old who has seen the world a bit, may make you make sense of it. Once we have identified them, it's time to detach, run away, let go, and never even start in the first place.

I am not going to give a point-by-point breakdown here. Because I feel it comes down to one basic tenet – know your worth. You don't need to be Michelle and Barack Obama to be treated well by your other half.

You don't need the anxiety, the constant stress, and the uncertainty. Please notice these signs, close your eyes, say a prayer of self love, remind yourself of how amazing you are and how you deserve amazing love. Or at least, a love that tries.

KNOW YOUR WORTH. AND ONCE YOU DO, BEHAVE LIKE IT.

10

Consent

(Shout it out loud – NO is NO)

We are living in the world post the #MeToo movement, and hence, we know how important consent is now more than ever. Lots of us have suffered in the past because we didn't even know what consent constituted of. And consent applies to both women and men – anyone has the liberty to say NO and should use that liberty as much as they feel they need to.

Consent is basically a 'permission for something to happen or agreement to do something.'

This means nothing in a relationship, or one-night stand, or fling, or date, or ... basically any part of your life, should happen without your explicit consent. Never succumb to anything thinking 'this is what you have to do'; do it if 'this is what you want to do'.

Let me tell you a story: Ananya was dating a boy. He came over one night. He sat in his car and cribbed about how hard his day was. Would she give him a blow job to relieve his stress? He kissed her and slowly guided her head to his crotch. She was confused, but didn't really know what was happening. She wasn't enjoying it, but it wasn't that bad. She would just get it over with. Later, she kept feeling like something was off. She has known this boy since school, they were old friends and he was supposed to be a nice guy! She would forget about this.

Let me tell you about another experience a friend had recently. She had been hanging out with a childhood friend, who seemed 'safe' and 'normal'. But then, he proceeded to message her one afternoon that he was horny, and that he was thinking about her giving him a blowjob in the lift, as his white cum flowed down her face.

My friend was shocked and asked him how he decided to send her these messages as they were friends, nothing more. He backtracked and said he was only figuring out if she was okay with it. But, shouldn't he have asked if she was okay with flirty, sex messages before he sent them, and not after?

This is such a common scenario that we don't even think of it. All of us have gone through versions of this.

That's because we don't think it through enough, and rather be slightly uncomfortable, than create a scene. I do also feel the perpetrator also in this case doesn't know or truly believe that they are crossing the line. So, both parties have to be educated about what consent is. As I write this, a female LGBTQI activist has been arrested for raping another woman.

Rape and sexual harassment has no gender, and everyone should be taught about consent, until it's hammered in.

It goes to show that anyone can be raped, even men. The recent show, *Bridgerton*, got into controversy as a female character dupes her male lover into cumming inside her. That, too, is rape because of the absence of consent.

We often forget that rape could happen to any human, and we must see it like that – a violation of basic human rights of consent and their physical boundaries.

Tara Kaushal has a lot to say on this subject; she has written a whole book on it! 'The most commonly accepted responses to conflict are fight and fight. One is taught that screaming 'bachaao, bachaao' at the top of your lungs while fighting or fleeing are the only ways to react to 'uncomfortable' situations. Actually, there are four responses, and include what is called friend/fawn – the attempt to befriend and flatter the aggressor to deescalate the situation – as well as to freeze. Once you do process what's happening, it's likely that your instinct will kick in and you will do the best that you can.'

For the one giving consent:

Be clear. Know what you are comfortable with, and not. As soon as you even slightly feel a pinch of weirdness inside you, stop. Say no. Think about it. Do it another day. Be very mindful that saying no is your right, and nobody has the power to make you feel bad about it. If you lose a lover/friend because you chose to say no, let them go. Somebody who doesn't understand personal freedom shouldn't be in your life. Say no, say wait, say let's not do this. You are responsible for your mind, body and heart. Take care of it.

For the one who hears the 'No':

Don't be Aziz Ansari. Let's rejig your memory about that case. An article on Babe.com said, 'A 23-year-old photographer gave details about her sexual encounter with the celebrity and how the night she expected to be one of the most memorable ones, turned into a nightmare. In the detailed account, Grace (a name given to protect her identity) recalls how her preferences weren't asked right from the moment her wine was poured to the time when she didn't feel comfortable enough to indulge in sexual intercourse and felt uncomfortable with Ansari's course of action and the moves he made. Throughout the article, she maintained that she tried to explain her discomfort using various non-verbal cues but Ansari didn't seem to care about it till the time she openly and clearly refuted with a No and decided to go home, after another "cringe-worthy" make-out session.'

Open your mind. Hearing no is not an attack on you, it's a personal boundary. Respect other people's feelings. Don't make anyone do what they don't want to. If you feel a hesitation on their behalf, ask them, "Are you uncomfortable?" Ask questions: Can I touch you there? How are you feeling? Should we stop? Should we go on? Are you sure? Listen to the answer and respect and embrace it. Don't attack the person. Don't belittle them. Don't make them feel bad for saying no. Don't curb their freedom and force them. Just don't.

Kaushal attributes the problem with understanding consent to gender norms: 'In general, based on existing gender norms, us women need to find our voices, and be a lot more assertive about what we want and what we don't want. Men need to hear – and listen to – women's voices. In addition, women are seen as sexual gatekeepers, men as sexual scorekeepers – and these are not roles we necessarily need to play.'

Exercise your consent, and listen to another's consent.

11

Can we all enjoy erotica; sometimes known as porn?

(Of course, we can!)

I got a question from a young listener once, and this is what she said. It read – 'Hi Aastha didi. So, I am 18-years-old and I recently had a weird experience. I caught my brother, who is only 14, watching porn. I stopped him, and now he is all awkward with me. Should I tell my parents? I don't know what to do as I am so confused. I am also very worried as I myself have been watching porn these days, and touching myself. Am I a bad person?'

My first answer to this would be: NO. YOU ARE NOT A BAD PERSON FOR WATCHING PORN. NEITHER IS YOUR BROTHER.

That's the truth. Watching porn could be a healthy, and safe way to fulfil your own sexual desires, and also find out what you like sexually.

So let me tell you a secret I have never, ever told anyone.

I am 39, and I started watching porn only a few years ago. And how? I did a story on the comic porn star, Savita Bhabhi. I found her fascinating – especially as she was a woman who took control of her sexual desires. Be it with her husband, boss, fitness trainer, pizza delivery guy, college students – Savita loved them all. She made me feel liberated.

We also have to see most porn for what it is – there are well-defined gender roles in the average porn film and everyone follows that. The woman is always the secondary character and the man has all the control. That's not the way sex (and porn) should be in the times we live in. Everyone needs to be equal, even as far as porn is concerned. Also, most of us don't have perfect bodies with big boobs and penises. Nope. It's far too perfect for anyone's taste.

Asa psychologist, Hvovi Bhagwagar encourages as well as cautions, 'Is porn healthy? That is a hugely debated issue. Psychologists haven't arrived at any one agreement on whether porn is harmful or healthy. My take: use common sense. If watching porn normalizes sex, reduces body shame or spices up your sex life (without making your partner uncomfortable), then it's obviously fine. But excessive porn consumption has a darker side to it – addiction, partner violence, unrealistic expectations and can turn into an insidious social menace.'

If you are using porn to find yourself, and explore your hidden desires, or figure out how you liked to be touched, then go for it! But here are some things you can keep in mind:

▶ Make sure you watch porn that you know is made with the consent of everyone in the clip. And how do you figure that out? There are many ethical porn sites that you can visit, which will help you make an informed choice.

▶ Do it in moderation. Too much of anything is harmful. Tell yourself that like that one cheat day, you will indulge yourself with some ethical porn once a week, for an hour. Set some limits.

▶ Don't expect your real-life sex life to be like the one in the porn movie. That's not possible, and neither should that kind of expectation be laden on to your partner. Your partner is beautiful and desirable as they are.

▸ But, you can ask your partner to watch porn with you. Maybe you guys will find something new to try out.

▸ See porn as an experience that can heighten your masturbation session. Don't ever lose contact or connection with your body – use it to explore your body and learn more about your desires.

▸ Know if you are doing it to fill a void – for example, is it because your partner doesn't satisfy you anymore? If yes, then try and solve the issue at hand.

The legendary Hugh Hefner, who made porn mainstream, once said, 'Part of the sexual revolution is bringing rationality to sexuality because when you don't embrace sexuality in a normal way, you get the twisted kinds, and the kinds that destroy lives.'

Watch porn, and promote ethical porn, if you know you and your relationship can handle it. Websites likes XConfessions, created by feminist filmmaker Erika Lust, show porn through an indie cinema lens. Dipsea is for those of you that prefer to listen to some saucy audio rather than watch raunchy videos, and my favourite is Make Love Not Porn, which has real-life sex that is 'silly yet beautiful'. It's focused on consensual and fun sexual exploration without the performative cliche scenes that you so often find on porn sites. If reading erotica is your thing, then Literotica is the one-stop-shop for you. In fact, during the pandemic, the website saw a big jump in their users!

Just make sure porn is the side dish, not the main.

SECTION 3
Relationship Sagas

Lots of people want to ride with you in the limo. But you want someone who'll help you catch the bus.

– OPRAH WINFREY

12

How do we know this is The One, though?

(And in the eternal question: Kis Ko kiss karoon?)

This is a very common question I get on social media: 'How do we know if the one we are with/or the one we love, is actually the one for us?' The easy answer to that is, we don't know. We can never know. Unless, you have a crystal ball and know how to use it …

But here, let me tell you a story.

Aastha met Kishore. Kishore loved Aastha from the first moment. She was used to bad boys and so she didn't really bother when a good boy actually liked her. Aastha treated him badly. But then the two started talking. And they laughed, oh, how they laughed!

And then Kishore laid down the law. He said to her, 'I can't be a friend. So, if you are not interested in me … let me know. We can end this.'

Aastha thought about this a lot. She thought of all the bad boys and all the heartbreaks. And now that there was this good man in her life, was she going to be foolish and let him go? No. She looked at him and smiled: Yes, I love you, too.

But it was only later when Kishore went over to Aastha's house, without even batting an eyelid, to meet her father, did she realize that he was the one. It proved that actions spoke louder than everything.

If you didn't realize it, this is my own love story.

So, I would say this. You will never, in the beginning, know that someone is 'The One'. It will dawn up on you. It will be proved by every little action of theirs. That's how, as time goes by, you will know that this is it.

But, just in case you don't want to wait for the confirmation and for your gut to throw up a positive affirmation, here are some of the things you should look out for:

- **They are not scared to tell the world** – friends and family – that you are their SO.

- **They answer your call at 3 a.m.**, and will rush to help, no matter what.

- **They love you no matter** how you look – gorgeous in a little black dress or tuxedo or smelling of sweat in the morning.

- **They don't hide anything from you.** This could be a new friend they made, or the insecurities they have about their body or job.

- **They are not competing with you**, or are jealous of your success.

- **You trust them**, and there is no anxiety about where they are, or who they are with, or what they are doing.

- **Even after the worst of fights**, they still pick up your call and say, 'okay, how can we make this better?'

- **They may not agree with everything** you say (differing politics maybe), but they will keep it out of the bedroom and will agree to disagree.

- **They don't mind you being your own person**, with your own friends.

- **The one who genuinely knows what you do** for a living, and respects it.
- **The one who plans a future with you**.

'I think when you are truly able to be who you are with someone, your happiest and your ugliest version. When you don't have to shrink yourself to make someone else feel better. You know in your heart that you've found "the one."' Author Ishita Moitra makes it clear of how she know 'The One' is here.

You will never know who is the one for you, if you don't give it time and patience. Trust in the process.

According to Dhruv Sehgal, 'To be in a healthy relationship means you are being yourself.' Maybe that's how you know. When you are yourself in a relationship, that's the one to go after.

13

Can you smell and see the gaslight?

(Trust your gut, no matter what anyone says)

Gaslighting is a word we hadn't heard much before 2018.

In fact, it comes from a 1944 play and movie called *Gaslight*. In the movie, which is also the first artistic portrayal of this type of psychological abuse, a devious husband, played by actor Charles Boyer, manipulates and torments his wife, played by Ingrid Bergman, to convince her she's going mad.

Now, in 2021, the term is described as 'a form of emotional abuse, which is an act of manipulating a person by forcing them to question their thoughts, memories, and the events occurring around them. A victim of gaslighting can be pushed so far that they question their own sanity.'

Let's take some examples. Gaslighting is when someone constantly tells you things such as:

▸ I am not flirting with someone else. It's just your imagination.

▸ You made me get angry at you.

▸ It's your constant nagging that made me do something that hurt you.

▸ It's all in your head.

▸ You are overreacting.

▸ You like playing the victim.

It's basically all about undermining feelings and concerns to make them insignificant, and even make you guilty about ever having them.

Here's a story:

Aarti from Mumbai had been in love with a boy for six years. The going had been tough but after he had apologized for taking her for granted for many years, things had been getting better. He was getting better.

But then in 2019, things started getting bad; real bad.

He wouldn't pick up her calls, and he would vanish for hours. When she asked him what the trouble was, he would blame her for overreacting. When they fought, he would tell her he couldn't sleep all night as she had blamed him for something he had never meant to do. He called her crazy and a psycho.

Then, one day, Aarti saw his messages to another girl. He had been cheating on her for six months. Every time she seemed to be getting closer to the truth or suspicious, he turned it around on her.

Classic gaslighting.

I would say here that no matter how anyone gaslights you, or makes you wonder about what you are feeling or saying: always trust your gut. It's what it's there for. Never be afraid of being called a psycho, just because you are have a feeling something is wrong.

It's not always easy tackling such sitations. Actor Maanvi Gagroo told me, 'I would suggest other women to talk to a confidante in a situation like this. The one thing required in a situation like this is support because often victims start questioning themselves and that's detrimental not just to the victim but to other women in the future. Ideally every workspace must have a POSH committee, so to approach them and/or the HR department, is a good idea.'

The worst thing I can think about gaslighting is that it usually comes from people we blindly trust and love, and that's why it's so hard to spot it at first. But if you even feel a few of the indications I have highlighted above, please be on your guard and get ready to protect and heal yourself. If you won't do it, who will? Certainly not the person who is merrily gaslighting you into self-doubt and insecurity.

In Aarti's case, the boy had not only cheated on her but also made her feel guilty for feeling bad when he was ignoring her, in turn denying her, her feelings. Cruelty comes in many forms.

Once you have spotted a situation like the one I have talked about above, here is how you can deal with it.

- **Get in touch with the inner you**. Gaslighting makes us believe things about ourselves that are not true. We feel we are the aggressor, while we are the ones who are getting hurt. So, get to know what you really feel and ask yourself why you feel it to get to know the real reason behind your discomfort.

- **As I said, trust your gut**. I think deep-down inside we know when we are 'overreacting'. So, when you truly feel your instincts are warning you, trust them.

- **Confront the gaslighter**, and tell them you don't take kindly to being told your feelings don't matter. Tell them your concerns and ask them to respond. For your own good, distance yourself from the gaslighter.

- **See a therapist**, and ask for professional help.

- **Start believing in yourself, again**, by reminding yourself of all the good decisions you have made in your life. Know that your feelings and that your opinions matter – and you have the right to air them.

The last one is not a point. It's a life lesson. Love yourself. If you love yourself enough (and foremost – that doesn't mean you are selfish!), you will know when you are speaking your truth. Then nobody can deter you or tell you otherwise. Loving yourself will also ensure you can't take nonsense from anyone, but are also wise and smart enough to know what's a right battle to pick. When you react to the right things, you will know when someone is trying to push you off the right track.

Listen to the voices inside you. It means you are connected to your deepest self and that is your truth. A truth you need to follow. Or follow John Mayer's wise words: 'Keep me where the light is.'

14

So, you got cheated on. Now what?

(If Beyonce could stay with Jay Z, maybe you could forget, too. Or should you?)

Let me tell you a story. (Yes, I am going to get right into it).

Zahaan cheated on his partner Anya after seven years in a relationship. She had always known he liked being liked, but didn't know this was going to happen to her. He had also cheated on his ex, but their connection wasn't as great as Anya and his, right? Right??

Well, he cheated on her. With a girl ten years younger. With a girl who was young and thin. With a girl who, he said in a weak moment, seemed carefree.

Instead of leaving him, like his ex had, Anya decided to hear him out. To not leave and to give him another chance – less out of choice and more out of the fact that she couldn't even think of not having Zahaan in her life.

Both of them went on with life together. Anya thought of the other girl everyday – why did he choose her? Was she prettier? Was she thinner? Did they have better sex? Did she make him laugh more? Was she less of a nag? Did he have more fun with her?

And so Aanya asked him all these questions every day, and none of the answers pleased her. She still loved Zahaan but made him feel guilty every day. But, Anya didn't end it.

He heard her out everyday ... and he was truly sorry for what he had done. He had been seeking validation, and the fling had fed that need to be liked by someone younger ... much younger. Bringing the fling and the girl up every day and in every other conversation was making it harder. But he loved Anya, and he never wanted to let her go. Zahaan had promised not to give up this time or let her down.

As with Anya and Zahaan, who were struggling with this problem even a year after, getting over someone cheating on you is one of the hardest things a person has to do. It breaks them, and to put those pieces back together takes almost inhuman strength.

Cheating does come in many forms. It's not just about the physical act of having sex, but also emotional cheating. That DM you sent to someone on Instagram or the constant WhatsApp chatting into the wee hours of the night is also cheating if you have crossed a boundary. Think about it like this: What would you not like done to you, and then make that your boundary. Every time you talk to another person about your emotional problems or pour your heart out to them, instead of doing that with your partner, you might have crossed into the territory of emotional cheating. If you think another person is so attractive that you would want to be naked with them – well, some might think it is cheating. It really is about what boundaries do you set for yourself, or what you or your partner see as a breach of trust.

Also, some hookups are only for a night, while many go for months and years. There is a level of intensity that differs her, but at the end one may say: all cheating is cheating. You may have slipped one night, or you may be in love with the 'other', but all cheating is cheating. You need to be honest about why you cheated, and clarity should emerge.

The best way to do it is to end it, just like ripping off a Band-Aid. Both of you go your separate ways, as you set down the boundaries of what is okay and what is not for the both of you. You part ways and then heal in your own time. This sounds hard, and is to a certain extent, but at least you have decided to move on from someone who hurt and disrespected you. You have decided to start all over again. After a few months, in retrospect, most people who move on from cheating partners describe it as the best decision they ever made.

Here are some points you should be kept in mind:

- **Know that you can't do anything about it**. But what you can control is your new life. Asking why did what they did, is the wrong way of going about it. Cheater-free. Focus!

- **Stop thinking about the other woman/man**. Don't compare yourself to them. Easier said than done, I know. But think about this – in hating them, and comparing yourself to them, you are judging yourself. And you are better than that.

- **Take your time with the healing**. Days, months, years ... shopping, wine, vacations. Anything you need, do it. I have come to know that at these time, when you want to reject it the most, discipline and routine, come most handy. Get up, work, meditate, work out, and create. Don't lay in bed and mope.

- **Talk to a therapist**. Get everything off your chest without the risk of being judged.

- **Figure out what makes you happiest**; and do more of it. Discover yourself again. You do you!

- **Be gorgeous**, and successful. Nothing looks better than success as revenge.

But, in the harder scenario, that you do decide to stay with your lover – like Anya and Zahaan – forgiveness is the first step. Or at least, the intention to forgive. You have to be very clear, that one day in the future, you want to get over the fact that your lover once had sex with someone else. That they laughed with someone else or held hands with someone else. It will be a hard pill to swallow but if you have made up your mind, then good on you.

Whichever party you are, do these, and you should be fine!

- This goes without saying, but let's say it – the cheating has to stop. It can't happen ever again, ever, ever, ever again.

- There needs to exist total honesty – about who their friends are, who are they chatting with, who are they meeting ... no lies, no secrets. Tough titties!

- The top point will continue till trust is built up again. The cheater has to think of innovative ways to build trust. And that includes always, and ever, being around. No shady business! No vanishing! No ghosting! No lying! No more excuses!

- Answers should be given. Why did they cheat? It will be hard to admit these reasons, and even harder to hear these reasons, but it has to be done. Figure it out. And then work on the underlying reasons that one person felt the need to cheat. If issues are not addressed, they will raise their ugly head again, for sure.

- Commit yourself to starting over again. Forget (the act, not the lessons it taught you), forgive, and remember why you love the person in the first place.

It will make you feel just like what actress Eva Longoria once said: 'It wasn't about who he chose. I had moments of like: "Okay, I'm not sexy enough? I'm not pretty enough? Am I not smart enough?" Then I immediately stopped. No, no, no – don't start doing that!" Because you can get stuck in that cycle and you can carry that onto other things.'

Being cheated on attacks our core personality and belief system. It makes us stop believing in love. It makes us very insecure. That's why you must be very sure of what your course of action must be moving forward. I would suggest a clean break, as it's less messy, and take away the toxicity from your life right away. It's easier to deal with heartbreak when you don't have to see the heartbreaker every day.

On the other hand, moving on and giving a person another chance is truly a noble, selfless, and loving act. And you are a super hero for even trying it. If your relationship can survive this (and both the cheated-on party, and the cheater, suffer the pain), then it could really go the distance.

Love is always worth trying anything for.

Godspeed.

15

Just a reminder

This is something my boss, my mentor, once told me: 'Things, people, situations … you can get over it all. Stop. Switch off the button. And in a year, you will look back and laugh at why you thought this was going to be so hard. Actually a year could also be a week.'

16

Unlike Britney, don't be addicted to toxic

(What feels wrong, is usually wrong)

L et me go out on a limb and say that at least 75 per cent of relationships out there are toxic in some way or the other. And here I am not taking into account that half of the times even we don't know we are being toxic. So, if you look at it, maybe even 90 per cent are toxic. And only 10 per cent of relationships are full of lucky people who neither curb their partner's independence nor get their own rights trampled over. Okay, Okay, Okay ...

Let's start simple.

What is a toxic relationship?

As the host of a love and relationships podcast, you often find out that most people don't even know what a toxic relationship is. When Britney Spears sang about it years ago, we didn't quite grasp the meaning of it. We thought of it as a bad boyfriend, who cheats on a girl, or a bad girlfriend, who cribs every time a guy goes out with a girl, but it was more than that. It goes much deeper than that.

Toxic, a word that's become a part of our vocabulary, much after Britney sang about it, means 'poisonous', and first appeared in English in the mid-seventeenth century from the medieval Latin word *toxicus*, meaning 'poisoned' or 'imbued with poison'. In 2018, the Oxford dictionary named it the word of the year, as along with the #metoo campaign, toxic, too, had got sudden traction for different reasons – toxic masculinity, toxic environment, toxic work culture, and toxic relationship. These words were used heavily that year and have been ever since. It beat the word 'gaslighting', and I think that could be only because gaslighting is much a part of a 'toxic' relationship.

So, for me, the ideal way to describe a toxic relationship would be, a relationship that doesn't let one partner grow. It aims to spread anxiety, and makes you question every action you take. It makes you less sure of who you are and what your relationship status is. It makes you less you.

Okay let's break it down.

Serena Van Der Woodsen from *Gossip Girl*? Toxic. (Dan Humphrey always feels anxious and less than what he is around her.)

Bunny from *Yeh Jawani hai Deewani*? Toxic. (Naina has to always explain how she is as cool as him.)

Mr Big from *Sex and the City*? Toxic. (Even if we love him, he blows hot-and-cold making Carrie destroy all her other relationships.)

Kabir Singh. Toxic. Toxic. Toxic.

I would even say Rachel from *F.R.I.E.N.D.S* is also toxic.(She almost treats Ross like a standby.)

Well, you get my point.

As a psychologist, Bhagwagar sees a lot of toxic relationships in her client's lives. 'Most people, both men and women, assume a relationship is damaging only if there's physical abuse or infidelity involved. Wrong. The most toxic relationships are the ones where the partner gaslights, damages self-worth, and controls. Leaving such a partner is tricky because often you will be left doubting whether you are imagining the abuse. Listen to your body, if it doesn't feel safe around your partner, make the choice to quit. However tough it feels, or however little support you get.'

I have given you a few examples from popular culture but let's get into specifics.

Who is a toxic lover?

In a single line, it's a person who isn't good for you. And if you need a checklist to see if your partner is toxic, read on:

A toxic lover is someone who ...

- **Puts their own comfort and convenience** ahead of everything – especially you.

- **Never thinks of your work**, home life, career, or time.

- **Leaves you hanging and waiting** – emotionally and literally – and does it repeatedly.

- **Is never clear about their intentions** regarding you or the relationship.

- **Comes back to you** when they have nothing else to do or nowhere else to go.

- **Doesn't care** about your mental health.

- **Abuses you** verbally, physically, mentally or emotionally.

- **Doesn't trust** you.

- **You can't** trust them.

This list can go on, but I think by now you may have recognized if anyone in your life is toxic.

I had a breakthrough the other day and came up with a line that I feel sort of described why we have normalized toxicity; it's because we often mistake the anxiety that toxic behavior incites in us as the butterflies in our stomachs – which is perceived as romantic. But it's far from it. We think that when we fight, and make up with sex, without addressing the issues, it's passion. When we believe every lie, because love changes people, and we mistake it as true love. It's not love. It's getting taken for granted. Start normalizing feeling comfort instead of anxiety.

There is a meme on Instagram that shows a girl standing in front of a door that says, 'Red flags ahead', and she says, 'Oh that doesn't matter to me, as I can't read!'

It's funny and also familiar, and also really tragic that we go willingly into such relationships. Maybe because we crave connections?

Let me tell you a story.

One of my podcast listeners, Manav, had fallen in love with a girl who he knew was bad news from the start. She had an ex she wasn't over, she never acknowledged Manav publicly and she came over when she wanted to but he could never call her. It reminded me of the time Mr Big dated a model in '*Sex and the City*', and says, 'She can always call me, but I can never get her.' Manav felt lonely and upset every evening but continued to be with this woman.

To give you more perspective, let me tell you about my first big love …

He led me on by telling me I was different and he made me meet his parents, went and hung out with my friends behind my back, and made out with my college best friend. He hated my friends. He used to get upset if I chose to spend time with my family or friends over him, even once. He even took the change, after I paid the bill! He went to the USA to study and then one day just stopped picking up my calls.

I saw all this happening, and I still went out of my way to love him and be there for him. In the end, it was a big, huge heartbreak.

And though you forget all the heartbreaks soon enough, why not avoid them? Or at least walk into them with eyes wide open.

Here is a mini list of sorts, of the red flags that will help identify a toxic person:

- **They will never be available** when you need them.
- **They will avoid you** if they have something more exciting going on.

- **They will make you question** your appearance.
- **They will be interested in other people**, and ensure you know of it in some way or the other.
- **They will gaslight** you.
- **They will avoid fights** by charming you, or having sex with you.
- **They will take** you for granted.
- **They won't spend too much** time, effort or money on you.
- **They don't let you** be you.

You get my drift.

Writer and journalist, Tara Kaushal sees toxicity in relationships as … 'Experts say – and I concur – that our model for relationships is backwards, that we expect an idyllic 'honeymoon' period and for conflicts to arise later. Actually, angry and honest conversations in the beginning can lead to a healthy relationship with not a lot of fighting later on. So, unless the fighting is vicious and/or physical, don't be too quick to dismiss a conflict-ridden relationship as toxic. Other signs of an unhealthy relationship can be apparent straight off, of course – jealousy, controlling behaviours, sexual violence, different morals, etc.'

Dear reader, the point to know is this – you know deep inside what is toxic and what isn't good for you and your growth. Don't ignore these signs, just because you feel like you won't find someone. I truly believe it's better being alone, than being with a toxic person. That being said, there are billions of people on this planet, and choosing a toxic person to spend your time with means you don't trust the magic of the universe.

Love yourself and give no space to toxicity in your life.

Now that we have figured out how to recognize what toxic relationships and people are, let's figure out how to leave such a relationship and how to win back your confidence after that! Kaushal says, 'Economic independence is necessary to exit a toxic relationship, particularly a marriage. (Familial support would be a bonus.) So many things that we perceive as acts of bravery – like leaving a relationship, job or man at the altar, or starting a business, fresh new life, etc. – boil down to money. Once that's in order, you'll have an easier time getting out.'

17

How to move on

(In life; as well as on Instagram)

As I am writing this, I got another great idea for a podcast – things that the 90s taught me. Well, along with the fact that Uncle Chips are the best chips, and that life was better off without a mobile phone, it also taught me that breaking up was so much easier back then.

Let me give you a personal example.

I was dating someone. We had a bad breakup. His ex called me, blah blah blah. I went over to pick up books and CDs – for the uninitiated, CDs were Rs. 395 a pop back then – I had lent him. And to give back the stuff he had given me. I took my embarrassed best friend, knocked on his door, gave him his things, saw the ex peeping from the bedroom, scowled, and left without a bye.

That's it. We were done. I fretted and fumed for a day. That's all.

Even I am amazed how easy it truly was.

The lack of any social media and online common friends made getting over an ex as easy as eating cake. Of course, you felt pain, rejection, resentment and all that other stuff, but I think you didn't dwell on it as much. But these days, it's a task.

People move on right in front of your eyes – the eyes that are stalking their Instagram feed closely; eyes that see every move and then cry over every move. It's hard to move on these days. I get many youngsters writing to me and their only question again and again is, how do we get over someone? I say, be creative, focus on work ... and they say, but how? But I can see their new girlfriend. But they look so happy. But they don't care about me?

Sigh.

It's hard to move on. I know. I know. I know.

But the point is to try.

We need to try to move on till it becomes muscle memory. It becomes a habit, and soon, you can be objective and look at the past and think, and know deep inside your heart, that all that happens, happens for turn over good.

But how to get there could be a hard battle. But we can suit up, right?

Actor Harleen Sethi, who recently featured in the series *Broken yet Beautiful* which was all about the ups and downs of millennial love, told me how she feels about heartbreak: 'Heartbreak does not always have to be associated with negative feelings … it can be a great time for growth, both personally and professionally. Moving on happens with time when you put full faith in the universe that it's all working out for your betterment and maybe you don't see it right now but God knows it best because God is seeing the bigger picture. You got to surrender to life and keep finding positive ways to swim through the unknown. Use affirmations and become grateful every time you feel low or victimised or feel too much pain. Everything passes – the good times and the bad. So let it pass, try and indulge less in what happened and why it happened, the deeper you dig, the messier things get in your head, so let the thoughts come and let them pass and that's the only way to move past it … the operative words being TRUST and SURRENDER.'

So, putting all my knowledge to use, especially the wisdom I picked up growing up during the 90s, is that the first thing to do is to cut all communication. Distance, in this situation and invisibility makes sure your heart forgets, instead of growing fonder.

So, the first step would be to unfollow, and block, on all forms of social media. The blocking doesn't mean you hate them. It just means that even if you are tempted to see them, you will have to go through the whole process of unblocking. So, block them for your own good.

Secondly, tell all your friends who may be following the said person, to not ever, ever, ever tell you what the person is upto. You don't need to know if they got a haircut, if they were dining in your neighbourhood restaurant, and if there is a new girlfriend/boyfriend on the scene.

YOU DON'T NEED TO KNOW.

Thirdly, block them on your phone, and messages. You don't want to message them, and you don't want to receive messages. Not until you have the ability to reply in a sane and sorted way.

But these are very practical, tangible things to do; the real key is to move on in your head and heart.

And that's when the real work begins.

I think the key is to remind yourself why you can survive without your lover. Remind yourself that people come and people go, but you can't let that diminish your glow. Tell yourself that as much as you loved them, or they are attractive (if you think that there is no one else who can turn you on like they did), you can produce that much love for yourself too. If their smile or touch turned to you to mush, it's time to find that same love for your own smile. It's very, very hard, but you have to be enough for yourself.

Often, our body cripples with pain because we think we can never feel the same emotion and intensity for someone else – I don't know if we can. I think sometimes we feel what we feel for that one person only. But I also do know that the human spirit is equipped to handle the gravest of trauma. This is just a person not loving you anymore. You will be okay.

Imagine what will happen if you took all of this energy and put it in your own work and well-being? You will level up like never before.

Like the great, and my favourite, writer Haruki Murakami said, 'Pain is inevitable, suffering is optional.'

So, here's what we do.

> **Know that this may take a bit of time**. There may be times you are sure you are over your ex, and one word, one movie, one song, or even a whiff of a perfume, will take you back. Be kind to yourself. It's not a weakness to miss someone.

> **Accept what happened**, and try and not carry the resentment ahead. Sadness, grief, anger, there will be a gamut of emotions you will feel. Feel it once and for all. If that means you cry in bed for a week, so be it. There will come a day, when the

sun will be shining outside, and you will see it telling you to get up and get going.

▸ **Whatever happens, happens for a reason**. It's such a big cliche. But it's so true. This person isn't for you. Your journey of love doesn't end here. The world is your ocean. Swim along.

▸ **Let your friends make you feel better**. Go out. Have fun. Laugh. Dance. Embrace life.

▸ **Forgive your ex**. Sometimes, people don't mean to hurt you, they just do. And even if they did do it on purpose, now that you have left them behind, let the pain be left behind as well. Ask yourself if you learned a lesson; for example, if you didn't trust your gut instinct last time, maybe going forward, you will listen to it.

▸ **Work on yourself**. Join a yoga class, learn meditation, join a gym, learn the ukelele, sing, learn how to pole dance, travel, cut your hair, learn Italian in preparation for your Italian vacation.

▸ **Do the things you love**. Whatever it is that brings you the most happiness, do it again and again.

▸ **Meet new people**. But don't try and fill a void. You are a whole person, regardless of who is in your life.

▸ **Know and believe** that there is nothing wrong with you. Things don't work out. It's the way of the world.

▸ **Things will work out** – believe in that. Be receptive to love. And let it in.

Only love fills the void left by love.

18

Long-distance relationships

(Love can travel nadiyon paar. That is, if you want it to)

This is a tough one. But then most questions about love are tough.

Also this is tough, especially for me. I need tangible proclamations of love. I need to be around someone, meet someone for lunch and dinner, kiss, cuddle, talk about what's happening at work, have a drink when there is something to celebrate, have a drink when you need a cry. I need someone to fight with, raise concerns, shout, scream, and then cool down and make up.

But who said we can't do all that and still be miles apart? Especially in today's world.

When love is so scarce and with so little to go around, when you find it, you can't let it go. Even if it's long distance. Actually, especially if it's long distance. Are you really telling me that you are going to let go of a person who loves you, just because they decided to move away for a while?

Not at all.

But of course, we need to work on making sure the long distance doesn't become an impediment.

Also, if you are a certain type of person, it will work out slightly better for you, though I feel like if you really like the person you're with, we can all try and be the type for whom these relationships will work.

Who is the long-distance type?

▸ The trusting one

▸ The trustworthy one

▸ The secure one

▸ The not-easily swayed one

▸ The one who doesn't need constant validation

▸ The one who can stick to a schedule

▸ The one who can be spontaneous

▸ The patient one

▸ The one who is okay with not having too many options on the menu

Isn't the last one funny? I am quite proud I thought of that one. LOL.

But it's true! If you want to weigh your options and try and date as much as you want before you settle down, then a long-distance relationship won't be an ideal one for you.

Then, it's better that you get onto a dating app and date around so you can make your choices in a more informed way.

But, if you match with even 70 per cent of the points listed above, then I think this can work for you.

As Margaret Atwood said, 'I exist in two places, here and where you are.' Isn't that such a lovely way to put it? So, let's see how you both can exist, without breaking apart.

▸ So let me tell you about a friend of mine, Aman. He was trying a long-distance relationship. Now, Aman had a very demanding job. Out of the house at 9 a.m. and back only by 10 p.m. Eat, change, go to sleep. Now, I asked him what I think his girlfriend also asked him: 'When did he have the time to talk to her? Facetime her? Call her? Text her?' Turns out he didn't have time to do any of that. It wasn't his fault. But neither was it hers when she decided this wasn't working for her. And, so, the first very important point is to figure out your schedules. And also, make sure your partner is okay with your schedule.

If you do have really busy days, and can't make the time to video call every day, or even once a week, then it's better to be upfront about it. If you are so tired by the time you reach home that you can't even have a good texting session, then say it out loud. If you are in different time zones and it feels like a chore to get up and sync out a time that's good for you both, then this is not meant to be.

So, sync your schedules. Make time for each other. When you are having fun, even a lot of it, remember there is someone thinking of you. Message them. Tell them you had a great time, and you wanted to share your experience with them. Share your life, send pictures, make calls, and make surprise trips. But, most importantly, tell them when you aren't having fun. Tell them when you are in a bad mood. Tell them about your failures. So that they don't feel you are ignoring them even when you are just moping. As The Plain White T's sang in '*Hey There Delilah*': 'Don't you worry about the distance; I'm right there if you get lonely.'

▸ Know clearly what the end goal is. Is this a trial period? Are you in it for keeps? Are you going to get married? Or is there a live-in relationship at the end of the tunnel? Also, are you sure this long-distance is not making you pull your hair out? Keep talking to each other, so that you both know you are on the same page.

▸ It's not all about texting. Call and please visit. Technology is a bitch sometimes and very detached. Write letters, send gifts and hop on a flight for a surprise visit.

▸ I have always felt this about conversations – asking what you ate, what you did in a day are very basic things, and will eventually bore the both of you! So think about the important stuff and talk about those. It will improve the quality of your conversations. Also, when people move away, they discover new things – so why not ask them about that.

It will be like the first few times you spoke in the early days of your relationship – when everything was about, what music do you like, what TV shows did you watch, what is your favourite book these days; everything was so interesting then, remember?

▸ Build trust. And believe in the other person. When you feel like flirting with someone, stop. You have a beau. Remind yourself that trust is everything. If you found out they were doing the same thing, you would be hurt ... very hurt. So don't lie, don't cheat, don't do anything you wouldn't have done to you.

▸ Keep going on with life – grow, expand, find and discover new things, people, become a new person. Doing that doesn't mean you won't be true to the person you are with. Not putting your life on hold means you won't resent the person you are with, and you will know that you are a whole person by yourself.

▸ Be positive. Be happy. Know why you are doing this. Believe in your love. Believe that you will make it through.

At the end of it all, I will say it again: Once you find love, don't give it up. Distance is ... well, just flights, ships, cars, and steps away. Didn't you hear? Love even moves mountains and oceans? Say it again and again ...

19

Marry to have fun!

(Yes. That's the best advice I can give)

Yikes, so if all goes well, you end up married.

Now that you have read the 'How to know who is the one' chapter and got together with them, and remained with them for a while, you may be ready to pop the question, or answer the question.

But how to know you are truly ready for marriage and what to keep in mind once you are married? Let me start with the first one.

There is no way to know you are ready for marriage. If we keep thinking about when we will be ready, we will never get married. Marriage is an engagement of love, and to overthink it, is going to take the fun out of it. So don't overthink it, and know that you will never surely know if you are ready for marriage.

> But here are some ways you can know, at least to be sure you won't run away from the wedding:
>
> - **You know you are not doing it** because you have to do it. You are doing it because you want to be with someone you love, or want a life with.
>
> - **You are not doing it to seek validation** – that you are worthy! Nope. Please be happy with yourself, single, before you get married.
>
> - **You aren't getting cold feet**. To be honest, I got married because I didn't even feel one second of apprehension after I had agreed to my husband's proposal. So, if you feel even uncomfortable even once, think about it.
>
> - **Maybe your friends and family** can sign off your choice too. They know you well enough and will know if someone is right for you. Do listen to them, just enough to take an independent decision. You know that friend of yours your mom never liked? In retrospect, you don't like them either. I think I made my point.
>
> - **You can say sorry**, and you can work on arguments and fights. If you are going to run

away at the first big fight, let me break to you, marriage is not meant for you. You need to work things out, instead of walking away.

- **You are okay with the initial passion** wearing off. You realise that true love is about companionship and respect.

- **It's about balance**. You and your partner are on the same level, and nobody has an upper hand. Perhaps you felt it was all about you when you were 21. Not now!

- **Unless you are very young**, make sure you are happy with your job, and are earning enough to fend for yourself. My husband and I were both earning barely 30k per person. But we knew we were going to grow together, and now when we are almost in our forties, we can be okay with the bad financial days, and not judge each other. But if you are above thirty, then only get married if you are both financially stable (enough to get by), and are in the job you see yourself growing in.

- **You are not setting out** to have the perfect wedding with the perfect person. You are going to be taking a journey with someone that's going to be imperfect, but it's going to be amazing!

Once you have got all the points down pat, go get married! And once you are married, please work on it daily – like brushing your teeth.

Marriage is hard work. But it's also a lot of fun. It's really nice to have someone waiting at home after a long hard day, who gets you a packet of chips and a bottle of Thums Up and gives you a foot massage. It's really nice to know that no matter, there is someone who is on your side. Choose well, choose wisely, and know that if it doesn't work out, it's okay. Love is never bad.

I asked bestselling romance author Durjoy Datta and his wife Avantika Mohan about their secret to a great marriage – one that transcends happy posts on Instagram. Datta said to me, 'To make a marriage work, just keep grinding at it. It's easier to stop working at it. So, I think resilience is most important.' While Mohan feels, 'One needs to keep the conversation going. That's the most important part. Rest everything can be rebuilt, but conversations.'

20

Is your lover also your best friend?

(Soulmates exist, but there are many of them, in many forms)

Ioften find it amazing when people expect their partners to be all they wanted and more. He/she has to be good looking, smart, kind, funny, loyal, interesting, sorted, have a good job, love everything you love, and vibe with you on each and every level. What??

Was this person created in a lab? How are they going to be this perfect? If you expect too much from someone, what you will end up with is a lot of disappointment. And resentment.

So, here is what we do.

We love our lover for who they are, and for all the other stuff they may be lacking, we fulfil those criteria in our friends.

Before I explain how we can do that, I just want to say here: Honey, it's okay if your honey has other friends – boys or girls. As long as they are just friends, which most of them are, there is nothing to worry about. Nobody can take your place. Okay?

Okay. Now, let's move on, and as I explain things you will know what I said is right on point.

So for me, my other friends are…

- K, with whom I talk about the universe, magic and watch the world go by.
- A and P, with whom I drink wine as we make sense of everyday life, love and work.
- N, who I talk books with. And who will always give good advice about work.
- N, who I gossip with and get musical with.
- A, who I talk about 'Love Aaj Kal' with.
- S, we talk about growing older and remind ourselves what we were and what we are now.
- N, S and N, who have known me so long now that they have a hand and a ring-side view of how I have turned out.

▸ M, who is my biggest supporter, and vice versa.

▸ And, finally, Kishore, who is there, no matter what.

It is because of all these people that my romantic relationship could be a solid one. And it's precisely why we need friends.

Friends are there to cheer you up when you are having relationship problems. And also remind you if you need to hang on or bow out. Your good and well-meaning friends will always give you a different perspective, that will mostly make sense. Their advice will always be well-intentioned, and you are better off for it, even if you don't end up taking it.

▸ Friends take the sorrow out of any situation. They will make you laugh and dance with you.

▸ If your relationship is long term, there will be times when you fight or have painful moments. When that happens, it's much easier to make it through if you have friends around for help.

▸ It's not possible for your partner to like to do all the things you like to do. So if they want to go to an open mic, and you cringe at the thought of it, it's better they go with a friend. If you want to kill zombies at a VR arena, then you better have a friend for that too.

▸ You need connections that aren't only romantic, and your friends will provide you with close-knit bonds that will ensure that you are a more sorted, and well-rounded person.

There have been so many movies and stories written on friendships that it is not a surprise that Rangita Pritish Nandy, producer of the series *Four More Shots Please!*, had much to say to me about this.

'A girl needs friends. Sisters. Relationships, lovers come, hopefully stay, definitely go but a girl always needs friends. For when she needs to come up for air, for when she needs anchoring, for when she's feeling ugly naked and wants the lights off, for when one bottle of red seems like a drop, for when she needs an honest, sane word in a lonely, confusing and terrifying pandemic. Sure, sometimes you get lucky and a lover can be some of those things but if you're luckier, you'll have that one friend or a tribe who'll be your home. This last year, I haven't missed a lover but there were days when I ached for my people. That's gotta be special!'

What Rangita says goes for men and their friends, too. Everyone should have good friends! So, have your own friends. And, let your love have theirs. And maybe all of you can be friends, too!

If you don't believe me, at least listen to Dhruv Sehgal, who wrote and acted in the sweetest very-real romedy of our times, *Little Things*: 'There are different sources of happiness and to put pressure on love to give you that happiness is just unfair.'

Just be.

21

Intermission

(The A to Z of the L-word)

It's the midpoint of this book, and I feel like I have so many random thoughts about love, that I just want to say them out loud.

a. Love is the bag of chips and Thums Up your partner has waiting for you at home when you get back after a hard day.

b. Love is knowing that no matter what, beyond the good looking boys and girls, your partner only feels desire when you stand next to them.

c. Love is knowing someone cries when you cry.

d. Love is knowing that this one person will text you back, and call you back, and just be there for you.

e. Love is when the person who is sleeping next to you says they want to drive away somewhere, but not without you.

f. Love is when someone has sex with you, and it feels like a part of their soul stayed with you.

g. Love makes you feel safe – about being the true you.

h. Love means you are happy when the other person is happy.

i. Love is being apart, and still loving each other.

j. Love is never making the one you love question if you find them attractive.

k. Love means never letting the one with you feel anxiety – they should never be standing in the middle of the road wondering what they did wrong, for you to block them out of your life.

l. Love means your partner loving your parents.

m. Love means someone who will never get bored with you.

n. Love is someone who misses you when you even fly out for a night, because the bed seems empty.

o. Love is someone who wants to go places with you.

p. Love is someone who waits with you in a bookstore/hardware store just because you want to browse there for hours.

q. Love is chai, ready and made.

r. Love is believing you even if what you say sounds made up (I saw aliens in the bathroom/I got sexually harassed by my boss).

s. Love is being so silly and uncensored that sometimes you wonder how you even ended up with them (Talking with food in their mouth/ farting in funny ways). Really?

t. Love is fighting about the smallest of things, but forgetting about it soon enough.

u. Love is eating carbs together.

v. Love is working out together.

w. Love is picking up after each other.

x. Love is looking around frantically in a crowd when you lose them.

y. Love is finding them and acting as if you have seen them after a 100 years.

z. Love chooses you. Every damn time.

22

Friend-zoned

(The worst place where love goes to die, is a place you can escape)

Oh, it's sweet misery to be friend-zoned.

Let me tell you a story (I really do seem to have a lot of those!)

Once, I was friends with a lovely boy. Akshay was intelligent, and listened to great music (and had a great CD collection). He was also kind, sensitive – a good guy through and through. I used to love hanging out with him. And I felt myself with him. But I wasn't attracted to him. And so, I friend-zoned him.

But as I spent more time with him, I found myself reevaluating my feelings for him. Because, inside, innately, I had always believed that you like someone for the way they make you feel.

But I was too late.

I had hurt him by friend-zoning him, and so he started believing that I was using him. So, the day I did decide to tell him that I liked him, he told me to get lost (he wrote me a lined typed letter, that reminded me that even though I was amazing and gorgeous, I was full of myself and he didn't like me at all). So, he became the one who got away.

For me, friend-zoning is a totally unnecessary act. Don't do it. You don't need friends who are in love with you, just because you think they will go the extra mile for you. This will lead to heartbreaks for the person who is being friend-zoned.

The solution is a simple one. If you think someone is interested in you romantically but you don't feel the same way, tell them clearly. Don't make them hang around and give them hope that you may change your mind. It may happen, but it may not.

People who are being friend-zoned, grow a spine, guys! Don't hang around someone who you fancy, just because you think they may see you in a different light. You are doing all they desire and are an instant ego-booster. What hanging around will do is that the person will start taking you for granted. If they have you around anyway, without the responsibilities of a relationship and of returning your love, then why would they ever want to change the situation?

Learn from Anjali in *Kuch Kuch Hota Hai*. The day she realises that Rahul isn't interested in her, she takes off. She starts leading her own life. And little do you know, he comes back trotting.

So, if you want to avoid being friend-zoned, here are some rules to follow:

- **Tell the object of your desire** that you like them early on. Don't wait around, or you may be waiting forever. Strike!

- **Set the rules down**. Don't be treated like a friend if that's not what you want to be. My husband told me earlier on that he liked me and he couldn't be *just* another friend, so I needed to make a choice, or say farewell to him. The threat and the clarity, worked.

- **Flirt, make romantic gestures**, be a lover boy/ lover girl – don't act or feel like a friend.

- **Don't be a pushover**. Be bold, say how you feel, and don't be a nice guy/girl at the cost of getting hurt or sidelined.

- **If you ask them out**, and they say no, let them know you will be moving on. And then, move on. Never stay where you are not appreciated.

Being a friend to someone you love is one of the hardest things one can do in life. Don't give yourself that pain. Only you can look after your heart best.

23
A reminder

-◆-

Your lover will cry. Will shit. Will shout. Will scream. Will call you names. Will annoy the f*** out of you. Will make you cry. Will look fat. Will look ugly. Will have dark circles. Will embarrass you. Will flirt with someone else. Sometimes. Will take you for granted. Will forget your anniversary. Will never do anything for Valentines' day. Will be selfish.

Sometimes, it's okay to let these flaws go. After all, we are all only human.

24
Epigraph

If all that I said in chapter 23 happens more than five times, end the relationship.

And begin again.

It's better to start a new journey, than to regret the time lost.

One day, you will find a better love.

SECTION 4

Love ain't always easy

Love is a verb
It ain't a thing
It's not something you own
It's not something you scream
When you show me love
I don't need your words
Yeah love ain't a thing
Love is a verb

—JOHN MAYER CROONING 'LOVE IS A VERB'

25

Another reminder

L ove sometimes is hidden in the person you never noticed, because you were so busy looking for your type.

It could be the boy/girl you grew up with.

Or the colleague who is always ready to work late with you.

Or the best friend who never lets you down.

Or the college mate who always waits for you after class, and then lends you their homework.

Or the boy you see every day at the station.

Or the girl who smiles at you every day at the grocery store.

Or the boy on Hinge you have friendzoned.

Or the girl on Tinder, who you treat as a booty call, but is the only one you are yourself with.

Sometimes, it's in plain sight in all these people.

You just have to open your eyes.

Did a bulb just go off in your head? *wink*

26

Being single is not a sin

(As Poo once said, 'Main apni favourite hoon')

RJ Rohini Ramanathan, who had once appeared on my podcast, was candid about how she handled being single after the age of thirty. She had been married once, but after her husband passed away, she had remained single for a few years. 'I think I finally got to know who I was, being single. I now know what I like, dislike, enjoy, hate … everything. I started paying attention to me, myself and I. And it's been a fulfilling journey. In fact, I got okay being alone, and that's not the same as being lonely.'

These can be inspiring words for a single person to hear, as being single is often considered synonymous with being lonely. Or being desperate, or being old, or not being good enough – in turn, it's almost considered a sin to be single, even by the most emancipated people.

I think being single, for both men and women, is not an issue to worry their heads about, only if they have broken their pre-conceived notions about being single. Society has made us believe that if we are devoid of a partner, our 'better half' is missing. What an utter load of crap!

You yourself are your better half, and an amazing, gorgeous whole.

But most of us feel like the *Sex and the City* episode, 'Bay of Married Pigs', where the conversation between the friends goes as (men, do your version of it!):

Charlotte: 'I hate it when you're the only single person at a dinner party and they look at you like you're a ...'

Carrie: 'Loser!'

Miranda: 'Leper!'

Samantha: 'Whore!'

Yes, single people are seen as sad, desperate, and always in search of a mate – who can blame them when every Hollywood movie shows singles out hunting for love? A 2008 study published in the *European Journal of*

Social Psychology found that people often think singles are unhappy. But, later studies have proved that this isn't entirely true, and mostly, singles seem to be doing quite well – researchers have actually studied them!

▶ Paul Dolan, a professor of behavioral science at the London School of Economics and author of *Happy Ever After* said, 'The happiest demographic might just be single, childless women.'

▶ A study by the *Journal of Social and Personal Relationships* said that being single actually increases social connections. Singles reach out to more social networks and give and receive more help from those contacts compared to their married counterparts.

▶ *Journal of Women's Health's* 2017 research suggests that unmarried people tend to be healthier. They exercise more and eat healthier. Single women had lower BMI and single men were less likely to suffer from heart disease. This could be attributed to the fact that they have more time to focus on fitness and food.

▶ A 2019 study published in the *Journals of Gerontology* (which studies the changes in our life through ageing), said that those who are single become more satisfied with their lives as they grow older.

Well, research seems to be saying only good things. Just like Charles Bukowski once said: 'There are worse things than being alone. But it often takes decades to realize this. And most often when you do, it's too late. And there's nothing worse than too late.'

Basically, what it means is this:

Being single ≠ being alone ≠ being lonely ≠ being desperate ≠ being unhappy.

In fact, real-life Carrie, Sarah Jessica Parker, said it well when she said: 'Being single used to mean nobody wanted you. Now it means you're pretty sexy and you're taking your time deciding how you want your life to be and who you want to spend it with.'

But all this is just talk if you don't know how to embrace single life.

- **Take a social media break**. Nothing highlights singledom as much as seeing coupled people all around. Especially when #couplegoals is making you gag more than a COVID-19 test. So, get off social for a while or hit mute or unfollow the accounts that are making you irritated. It doesn't mean you are a bad person, so don't go down a guilt trip. You are doing this for your peace of mind.

- **Make your goals and dreams the centre of your life**, not finding someone. Wake up every day and work on your life and that dream. If someone has to come along, they will, but you can't look for them or waste time looking for them.

- **Keep yourself occupied with the things that make you happy.** Running, singing, yoga class, travelling, or just going to parties and drinking wine, and dancing like no one's watching at these parties – do it all!

- **Don't equate sex with love, and love with sex**. But be truthful about your intentions, and less judgmental and touchy about someone else's intentions.

- **Learn the fine art of masturbation.**

- **Spend time with friends and family**, and everyone who loves you unconditionally.

- **Don't date just to fill a void**. Date when you find the person truly intriguing.

- **Learn how to be alone**. Light a candle, go shopping, get a pedicure, get a haircut, sit in a bar and drink an old fashioned, eat some cake at a cafe, watch netflix, watch a dirty movie and touch yourself, go travel to New York and spend six months there. Be happy with yourself.

- **Go on a lot of dates**. You are single, and ready to mingle. Be honest, and enjoy yourself. You have to kiss a lot of frogs sometimes to find a prince/princess.

Writer Sumukhi Suresh, like many single people out there, has found the way to tackle being single. 'As someone who is single, and anxious regularly about finding someone, I have realised that the more you think you think you need to work for love, it's going to run away from you. The best thing to do (and I know it sounds cheesy) is to like yourself. Spend your energy on liking yourself than hustling to get someone else to like you. The moment you chase anything, it moves away form you. It's also disrespectful to yourself, and your self worth. You don't like yourself, that's why you need someone else to like you. It's not an ideal world, but my advice is don't rush after anything , or else it won't come to you.'

Being single is truly a time to figure out your own life, without being worried about another's. But through it all, never stop believing and never slip into cynicism. Love is a wonderful emotion and seeing it in a positive light will even help you love yourself better. Take the example of something Jennifer Aniston told *Vanity Fair* after her break-up with Brad Pitt. When the interviewer asked her if she believed in love, she said: 'When I hear people say that they would never do it again, it's like cutting off your nose to spite your face.'

Now, why would you do that?

27

Does age matter?

*(Just don't become a version of your
moms and dads!)*

This is a tough question.

In love, nothing should matter, right? But let's talk about two scenarios.

Scenario number one: you are a woman in her forties, lets's say. And you are dating a man ten years your junior; how do you see him?

The lady is a boss woman and the man is trying to find out what he really wants to do; or be. He is initially attracted to her self-confidence and finds her inevitable trait of taking control sexy. She finds his innocence and lack of cynicism and worldliness refreshing. It's a hot situation for both of them and when asked 'Aren't you too old (or young) for him?' both just tell the world to sod off. Also, us women, too, see younger (and maybe good-looking) boyfriends, husbands, and our lovers as sort of trophy lovers. It's fun to have it all.

So, what happens in the scenario I described above? Do they last? I do hope they do.

I am hoping the same for our most awesome export to foreign shores, Priyanka Chopra and her husband Nick Jonas. They look happy together, but I have long learnt that what you see on Instagram is not always true.

In an interview to *Elle* magazine last year, Priyanka Chopra, who is thirty-six, said this about her relationship with Nick Jonas, who is twenty-six. 'People gave us a lot of sh*t about that and still do,' she said. 'I find it really amazing when you flip it and the guy is older, no one cares and actually people like it.' The singer has said he has found a muse in Chopra, and has said that any song that wasn't about her, just 'wasn't as good.'

Anyway, let's come back to the issue at hand.

So, few days go by fine; maybe even months. But then. The boss woman starts bossing the thirty-year-old 'let-me-figure-it-out' man. She buys him fancy stuff and plans his finances – well, she knows better and she just wants the best for him. But the moment he tries to do something by himself, she ends up feeling rejected. So, he now only hangs out with her and her friends and his life is truly fine-tuned to hers.

He, on the other hand, has become very comfortable in the life he has with this lovely lady who handles everything for him. All those plans he had made for himself are now out of the window – he had someone else planning his life now. But there was this niggling sense of resentment, one that came out of her always telling him what to do. But he can't leave her, that will mean to leave the comfort zone and become independent.

Phew. This is hard.

I hate to say it, but eventually either they live together in unhappiness forever as neither wants to change or one of them leaves the other.

Okay, scenario number two:

A thirty-five-year-old man, well-settled and moving along fairly smoothly in life, is dating a twenty-two-year-old. The girl is young, still figuring out what she wants in life, or love, or a man for that matter. Here she is, confused but there is this nice older guy who is suddenly wooing her.

This is what I think: He is going through a mid-life crisis, where women his own age seem to have too many wrinkles or too much make up, or love handles. This twenty-two-year-old (most probably) is flat-stomached, toned, young and less stressful. She doesn't even need him to treat her well; as long as he pays her some attention. This, my dear readers, is what a trophy girlfriend looks like.

She, on the other hand, is so happy someone is listening to her and is being in control. Boys her age have nothing much to say, leave alone take her out for a date to a nice place. And the sex is great – he actually knows what to do and even asks her if she had an orgasm!

So maybe this doesn't end and becomes a fulfilling relationship, which I hope it does. But mostly what will happen is that the twenty-two-year-old will discover that his older partner is toxic and really not as grown-up as she thought. He doesn't want a relationship, and eventually when she asks for all the things that a thirty-five-year-old woman wants, he will move on. And fast.

So, for me, age DOES matter. Because most people aren't well adjusted enough to not let it matter. Somewhere, somehow, age dynamics takes over, and one becomes bigger in a relationship than the other. And we all know, even if we haven't felt it, that balance is the key to a good relationship.

But if you are in any of these situations, this is what I think we can do. After all, all we want is for you to have a great relationship, and find love.

- **Don't let the age gap** make you feel like one is above the other. Always think about being equal in the relationship.

- **If you are older, stop yourself** from taking control of every situation.

- **Make all decisions together**. Think of it as one decision that will affect the both of you.

- **If you are younger**, don't ever see your older beau as your saviour from whatever you see troubling you.

- **If you are older, make sure** you encourage your young lover to follow their dreams. They need to come into their own, and not live in your shadow.

- **Don't be in awe of your lover**, by virtue of being older and wiser. Appreciate them but treat them as an equal.

- **Older or younger**, don't ever see your lover as a trophy – that gets old very soon.

Age may not matter, and it never has to. Love is what matters – but that only comes into play, if we let all the other stuff go. Put your ego and youth aside, and instead of following the rules that age brings, make your own rules. After all, you are only as old as you feel.

28

Polyamory: Do we need more than one lover?

(In an ideal world, I would have a list of them ...)

In one of the episodes of 'Love Aaj Kal', we had a nineteen-year-old, who was polyamorous. Now, as ancient as Ankit and I are, we were so surprised that such a nuanced (according to us) relationship type could be managed by a such a young person. Let's not get into if it's okay to call a nineteen-year-old a child – for anyone over thirty, a nineteen-year-old is a child. Anyway, here was this young girl telling us why she was good with polyamory.

For starters, what is polyamory? According to Wikipedia, polyamory (from Greek *poly*, 'many' and Latin *amor*, 'love') is the practice of, or desire for, intimate relationships with more than one partner, with the informed consent of all partners involved. It has been described as 'consensual, ethical, and responsible non-monogamy'.

Hmm. Well, what that basically means is that you can be with different people – sexually, emotionally, mentally – they all know that, and so it isn't cheating … and they all are okay with it. So, there is no heartbreak. At least there shouldn't be.

So, this is what she told us. She said she was in love once, but it didn't work out and was pretty painful. And so, the wise one that she was, she decided to not be in one relationship the next time – as in not putting all her eggs in one basket. And so now, she was mentally excited by boy A, sexually satisfied by Boy B, and emotionally fulfilled by Boy C. And everyone knew about everyone. It didn't mean that she cared less about one person, she liked all three. In fact, she had healthy, warm and caring relationships with all of them.

In fact, many anthropologists see polyamory as a natural state of being. Legendary French sexual therapist, Esther Perel's work draws on studies that demonstrate that women are not, in fact, biologically conditioned for monogamy: they are much more likely than men to experience a loss of sexual desire in long-term relationships and are more aroused by novelty than men. In fact in her book, *The State of Affairs*, she writes, 'The human imagination has conjured up a new Olympus: that love will remain unconditional, intimacy enthralling, and sex oh-so-exciting, for the long haul, with one person. And the long haul keeps getting longer. It's no surprise that this utopian vision is gathering a growing army of the disenchanted in its wake.'

They say it was the common way of life before the Agricultural Revolution. Ancient tribes existed in which sex was shared as commonly as food, even between people of the same gender. The paternity of children was a non-issue because there was no property to inherit and children were raised in common by the whole tribe. Arguably, since the above factor was absent and men didn't 'possess' women, there was no jealousy, fighting over women and abuse.

Doesn't that sound absolutely amazing? But wouldn't that be hard to do?

I, for one, wouldn't opt for polyamory. Love, universal as it is, is best felt in the romantic way with one person. If you love someone, you want to give them your all – emotionally, mentally and physically. If you had to divide all of these, you have friends for that – there is a friend who is the one you talk about books with; there is one whom you converse about the universe and its magical nature; there is another who you get drunk with and make bad decisions. But those are friends. Romantic love, for me, is ideal with one person.

Will Smith and his wife, Jada Pinkett Smith, said they were in an open relationship, and didn't want to avoid anything that 'happened naturally.' They said it didn't mean they didn't love each other. I guess they mean attraction and even the 'acting on attraction.'

The main question to ask is how do you get yourself to the emotional maturity where you are okay with your lover being sexual with someone else, or talking about their hopes and dreams with someone else.

But, there are always two sides of the coin. The journal, *Social Psychology*, suggests that polyamory means more relationships and that leads to more needs met. In the end, is it fair to laden one person with all your hopes and desires? Won't that lead to disappointment? The study continued to say that 'people in polyamorous relationships may better be able to experience both nurturance (the comfort and security associated with long-term relationships) and eroticism (sexual pleasure and passion associated with new partnerships) at the same time.'

But if you do decide to go with polyamory, as it seems simpler than a monogamy, please bear in mind four things: consent, trust, communication and mutual respect for everyone involved. A human heart is a fragile thing, and you would want to treat it well, even if you are not entirely responsible for it. Set down the rules, lay down the law, be as open as you can be, and then give all of these relationships the best of what you are in it for.

Remember what Carrie and Mr Big once said to each other, 'You create your own rules.'

29

Divorce is not the end

*(And the butterfly said to the caterpillar:
life begins again)*

Sometimes, marriage isn't the end of your romantic journey, and when that happens, it's okay! It's okay. Life goes on. Really, it does.

Of course, this is a major event. You have to change your life and start all over again. You will be full of doubts such as: were you not good enough, are you going to be alone for the rest of time, and what will people think of you. But you are strong: ladies and gentlemen, you can start over again, and you are going to be amazing and fabulous as you do it.

The reasons for divorce could go from simple to complicated. It could be that you didn't get along, or didn't have the same goals to work towards (like maybe having children), not being in love any more, not having great sex, or harder issues like toxicity, and physical, emotional and mental violence. But whatever the reason is, things end.

But as the chapter heading said, it's not the end.

So here is how you start over again.

- ▶ **Surround yourself with friends and family** and people who you feel comfortable with, and then ask for help, and let them take care if you. Also, get rid of the naysayers, even if it includes friends and relatives who are judging you.

- ▶ **Forgive yourself**, your partner and your marriage. Yes, it's damn hard to do that sometimes, but it's over, and now, you need to heal. The first step is saying it wasn't my fault, and if it was the other person's fault (which you think it may be), you need to forgive and forget, because it's the past. The past sucks, and it's no good keeping in the present.

- ▶ **Like all endings, try and figure out** what you can take from this in a constructive manner. How can you better yourself. And how can you use this to make yourself a more rounded person. I think getting to know oneself better is such an exciting thought. It's like being a teenager again, but with all the perks of being an adult.

▸ **It's true. A new haircut changes you**. LOL. But truly. Focus on yourself. Buy new clothes. Move a lot. Go on a vacation. Go to New York. Get on Tinder (maybe). But yes, go out on a limb. Do mad stuff yo!

▸ **Use all this extra time well**. Take a hobby class. Or meet all the friends you lost touch with.

▸ **Don't start obsessing** over the fact that now, you are going to be alone. Whatever age, size, place you are at, you will find love. It's inside you. You can never lose that. To think about a future that hasn't happened yet, in a negative way, may make it a negative future. So, do the opposite. Think as positively as you can – visualize the biggest, most badass and loveliest life you can! I promise it's going to come true.

Marriage is hard, divorce is harder. But I have truly written this book to tell everyone that love is not about these labels. It's not only found in marriage or vanishes with divorce. Love can be found anywhere – even in that geeky best friend from school, who is now a hottie!

Love is everywhere. Please don't get stuck up on labels and an image. Make your own way in this world of love at every corner. You can design it by yourself. Love is yours to mould. Now go out there and entice and flirt with love. It's already looking at you; sometimes in a satin-wrapped arrow or a thorn at the end of which is a beautiful rose.

30

Love is never bad

(An ode – it's time for one!)

The thing to realize is this.
Love is never bad.
Love didn't hurt you.

Maybe, love made you ecstatic,
It made you feel things you had never felt before.

Maybe, it made you open your heart,
And break down those walls.

Maybe, it made your body sway,
made it behave as if it needed another to survive.

Maybe, it made you feel like you could fly,
like you could finally make those dreams come true.

Maybe, it helped you open your eyes,
and see the world in a different light, a bright neon
    one.

The thing to realise is that love was never bad,
love never hurt you,
and if the one you loved walked away,
know that love worked exactly the way it should
    have,
because now you know,
you can do it all over again,
and you are even more amazing than you were
    before.

Love is never bad.

Epilogue

—❤—

I wrote this book to just put into words all that I have always been preaching. Love is meant for all of us, and love will find us no matter what. We just have to open up our eyes, minds and hearts to it. I feel as we let the daily strife and heartbreak get to us, we start finding comfort in letting ourselves believe that, love doesn't exist! But it does. It usually just arrives in a different form than you thought it would. But then, think about it. If you are so unique, then why wouldn't your love story be?

Keep your hearts wide open. Say, okay, I got hurt, but I will always believe.

I think it's easier than we think, if only we tried it out.
The world and the universe all want you to be happy.
Believe that.

Th next time a boy, or a girl, is reaching out to you,
put all your preconceived notions to rest, and think:

'What if I gave this a chance?'
'What if I gave myself a chance?'

And watch your world change.

Lots of love,
And good energy to all of you.

Aastha♥

Acknowledgements

I want to thank everyone who took time out to give their valuable inputs for the book: Rangita Pritish Nandy, Leeza Mangaldas, Dhruv Sehgal, Maanvi Gagroo, Hvovi Bhagwagar, Sumukhi Suresh, Tara Kaushal, Jyotsna Mohan Bhargava, Durjoy Datta, Avantika Mohan, Megha Rao, Ishita Moitra and Rohini Ramanathan.

This also includes all my friends who answered my questions patiently and candidly. Especially Devika Patel, who shared her love story with me.

Malaika Arora, Cyrus Sahukar and Durjoy Datta, thank you for reading the book and endorsing it.

ACKKNOWLEDGEMENTS

In the mad world we live in, to take out time for my book and I is truly a gift for me.

I want to thank Mohar Basu, for always being around to help and motivate.

And my editor Bushra Ahmed, who pushed with the right amount of love, persuasion and 'you-better-finish-soon-or-else' vibe.

Lastly, thank you to all the listeners of my podcast, who have shared their intimate secrets with me, which has led to the writing of this book. I owe you, guys.

About the Author

Aastha Atray Banan has been a journalist for 19 years and is currently the editor of *Sunday Midday*. She has previously published four romance fiction books, and this is her first non-fiction. Aastha wears many more hats other than being a writer; she has a hit podcast 'Love Aaj Kal' on Spotify India which deals with relationships and love, and has also written and released four original songs.

Made in the USA
Monee, IL
07 July 2026